*Twayne's English Authors Series*

Sylvia E. Bowman, *Editor*
INDIANA UNIVERSITY

*Leigh Hunt*

TEAS 210

J. Harter Del.        F. Wright Smith.

Leigh Hunt

# LEIGH HUNT

By JAMES R. THOMPSON
*Ohio University*

TWAYNE PUBLISHERS

A DIVISION OF G. K. HALL & CO., BOSTON

Library of Congress Cataloging in Publication Data


Thompson, James R.
  Leigh Hunt.

  (Twayne's English authors series  ;  TEAS 210)
  Bibliography:    p. 167 - 72
  Includes index.
    1.   Hunt, Leigh, 1784 - 1859—Criticism and interpretation.
PR4814.T47        828'.7'09          77-6803
ISBN 0-8057-6679-0

MANUFACTURED IN THE UNITED STATES OF AMERICA

To H. Glendon Steele
who introduced me to literature

# Contents

# About the Author

James R. Thompson is a professor of English Literature at Ohio University, Athens, Ohio. He received his B.A. and M.A. degrees from Bowling Green State University and his Ph.D. degree from the University of Cincinnati.

Professor Thompson has written and lectured on Byron, Wordsworth and nineteenth-century poetry; at present he is writing a critical study of the Romantic dramatic poet Thomas Lovell Beddoes.

# Preface

In the following study I assess as well as introduce Leigh Hunt, a man of letters both famous and infamous in his own age but often ignored or forgotten in ours. Since the decline of interest in the essay as an imaginative genre, Leigh Hunt has been lodged in odd corners of literary histories and of greater men's biographies; he has been kept alive by his extensive involvement with many writers of three vigorous literary generations. This involvement alone is worthy of rehearsal since the critic-editor who "discovered" and promoted John Keats and Percy Bysshe Shelley deserves recognition for his historical significance.

However, I have not concentrated upon that story, whatever its interest and importance; for the major focus of this study is on Hunt's direct and indirect contributions to the literature of his age: much prose and some poetry of no little merit; editorial and critical services of clear significance. For example, Hunt was one of the masters of nineteenth-century nonfictional prose, especially in the familiar essay which he helped pioneer. In such poems as his popular romance, *The Tale of Rimini*, Hunt assisted in the break-up of the old English heroic line and in the elimination of traditional poetic diction. As editor, he had a major role in the evolution of the modern periodical; moreover, as both editor and writer he set esthetic and moral journalistic standards that have had lasting and beneficial effects. Almost alone he transformed the theatrical review from a perfunctory, hypocritical and often self-serving notice into a respectable tool for dramatic criticism. As literary critic, he articulated the Romantic manifesto for a new and ever-widening reading public. These and other literary topics are the concern of this examination; and, beyond the first chapter, biography plays only a supportive role.

Hunt's writings are not only uneven and voluminous (more than fifty volumes would be needed for a complete edition) but also scattered throughout all genres. Consequently, I have chosen a categorical rather than chronological organization; but I have begun my discussion with poetry, his first literary endeavor, and concluded it with his *Autobiography*, his last major book and surely the most enduring. I comment on all his major creative efforts and significant literary activities through the discussion of his representative works. When scholars deal with such a prolific author, exhaustive treatment is, of course, impossible. My approach to his major written work is analytical and critical; to his other, but lesser, literary activities, descriptive. I have included as many samples of his writing as possible because such a practice is in keeping with an introduction of this nature and because it was Hunt's own chief critical method.

Numerous scholars, many of whom appear in my notes and bibliography, have contributed to our appreciation and understanding of Hunt. However, like all students of his work, I must especially acknowledge a considerable debt to Louis Landre's *Leigh Hunt (1784 - 1859); Contribution a l'histoire du Romantisme anglais* (1935) and to the three volumes of Hunt's essays edited and painstakingly annotated by Lawrence and Carolyn Houtchens. I wish to express my appreciation to the Ohio University Library for its procurement of a large collection of Leigh Hunt's first editions; to the staff of the Bodleian Library for many bibliographical contributions and much scholarly hospitality; and to Ohio University for a Baker Award freeing me for research. I also wish to thank my wife Janice, whose useful advice and unfailing good humor provided considerable support.

JAMES R. THOMPSON

*Ohio University*
*Athens, Ohio*

# Acknowledgments

I am grateful to the Oxford University Press for permission to quote from H. S. Milford's *The Poetical Works of Leigh Hunt,* and to the Columbia University Press for permission to quote from *Leigh Hunt's Dramatic Criticism 1808 - 1831, Leigh Hunt's Literary Criticism,* and *Leigh Hunt's Political and Occasional Essays* edited by Lawrence Huston Houtchens and Carolyn Washburn Houtchens.

# Chronology

1784     James Henry Leigh Hunt born October 19 at Southgate, Middlesex. Son of Isaac Hunt, American loyalist attorney who, escaping a Philadelphia mob, immigrated to England and became an Anglican minister.

1791     Enters Christ's Hospital School (in the footsteps of Samuel Taylor Coleridge and his future friend Charles Lamb). Refuses fagging; develops a taste for reading and writing poetry; leaves school in 1799.

1801     His early poetry is published by subscription in *Juvenilia*. Publishes article in the *Monthly Preceptor*.

1803     Engaged to Marianne Kent. Clerk in his brother Stephen's law office; clerk in war office. Serves as volunteer in the St. James Regiment.

1804     Assumes signature "Mr. Town, jnr., Critic and Censorgeneral" and writes for the *Traveller*.

1805     Becomes theatrical reviewer for his brother John's *News*.

1806     Edits five volume *Classic Tales* (1806 - 1807).

1808     Publishes *Critical Essays on the Performers of the London Theatres* ("1807"). John Hunt as publisher and Leigh as editor start the *Examiner* in January. The periodical is acquitted in the first of several prosecutions brought against it by the government. Leigh resigns post in war office; henceforth, a full-time journalist.

1809     Marries Marianne Kent. Father Isaac Hunt dies.

1810     Thornton Hunt born, first of seven children. Friendships with the painter Benjamin Haydon and publisher Charles Ollier begin. Starts the *Reflector* (1810 - 1811).

1811     Meets Percy Bysshe Shelley. *Examiner* prosecuted and acquitted. Publishes "The Feast of the Poets" in the *Reflector*, a poem satirical about most contemporary poets.

1812     John and Leigh Hunt tried and convicted for libel of the Prince Regent in the *Examiner*. Friendship with Lamb develops. Sentenced to two years in jail and fined ₤500.

1813     Goes to Horsemonger Lane Gaol where he entertains such notables as Lord Byron, Benjamin Haydon, William Hazlitt,

Charles and Mary Lamb, and Thomas Moore in his quaintly decorated rooms. Daughter Mary Florimel born in prison.

1814    Writes and publishes *The Descent of Liberty*.

1815    Leaves jail; meets William Wordsworth.

1816    Publishes *The Story of Rimini*, written in prison. Meets John Keats and sees much of Shelley. Prints his famous "Young Poets" essay (announcing Shelley, Keats, and the now forgotten John Hamilton Reynolds) and sonnets by Keats in the *Examiner*.

1817    *Blackwood's Magazine* opens its campaign against Hunt and "The Cockney School of Poetry."

1818    Publishes *Foliage*, an incomplete collection of his poems.

1819    Starts his *Indicator* (1819 - 1821); publishes *Hero and Leander* and *Bacchus and Ariadne*.

1820    Keats, suffering his final illness, stays several months with the Hunts but leaves after a quarrel.

1822    In May, Hunt family sails from Plymouth for Genoa. Shelley drowns in July shortly after Hunt's arrival. Stormy collaboration with Byron produces the short-lived *Liberal*.

1823    Friendship with Edward Trelawny. Byron joins revolution in Greece; dies there in 1824.

1825    Publishes *Bacchus in Tuscany*. Dispute with brother John over rights to the *Examiner* leads to prolonged break in relationship. Returns to London in December.

1828    Financial difficulty and resentment cause Hunt to publish his controversial *Lord Byron and Some of His Contemporaries* for which he is much abused.

1830    Brings out *The Chat of the Week* (June to August) and the *Tatler*, a daily paper running some seventeen months and written almost entirely by Hunt. Hazlitt dies.

1832    Receives royal grant of £ 200. Meets Robert Browning and Thomas Carlyle. *Christianism*, *Poetical Works* and his three volume novel, *Sir Ralph Esher*.

1834    Living near his friend Carlyle at Chelsea. Produces *Leigh Hunt's London Journal* (April 1834 - December 1835).

1835    Publishes his long antiwar poem *Captain Sword and Captain Pen*.

1837    Becomes editor of *Monthly Repository* (until April 1838).

1839    Friendship with Charles Dickens.

1840    Hunt's play *A Legend of Florence* successfully produced at Covent Garden. Publishes *The Seer*; edits *Dramatic Works of Sheridan*, *Dramatic Works of Wycherley*, etc.

1843   Publishes *One Hundred Romances of Real Life*.

1844   Sir Percy Shelley grants Hunt ɤ 120 annuity. Publishes *Imagination and Fancy*.

1846   Publishes *Wit and Humour* and *Stories from the Italian Poets*.

1847   Hunt's chronic financial difficulties eased by a ɤ 200 Civil List pension and by the proceeds from a benefit performance of *Every Man in His Humour*, acted by Dickens and others. Publishes *Men, Women, and Books*.

1848   Still alert for new talent, Hunt endorses and advises Dante Gabriel Rossetti. Brother John dies. Publishes *The Town*.

1849   While at work on autobiography, edits *A Book for a Corner* and *Readings for Railways*.

1850   Publishes *Autobiography*.

1853   Hunt is satirized as "Skimpole" in Dickens' *Bleak House*. Publishes *The Religion of the Heart*, a revision of the earlier *Christianism* (1832).

1855   Nathaniel Hawthorne visits Hunt at his Hammersmith lodging. Publishes *Stories in Verse; The Old Court Suburb*.

1857   Marianne Hunt dies.

1858   Play "Lovers' Amazements" produced at the Lyceum.

1859   Contributes papers to the *Spectator* (January-August). Dies at Putney, August 28, and is buried in the then model Kensal Green Cemetery.

CHAPTER 1

# The Man

## I *Reputation*

IN a modest corner of Kensal Green Cemetery in northwest London, Leigh Hunt's memorial bust gazes serenely out over a shabby burial ground and at the encroaching urban blight of the once attractive suburb. Except for a few of his possessions gathered at the Keats House in Hampstead, no other memorial to him exists in the London he so long inhabited and so often celebrated in his writings. Similarly, his admirers must comb the back-street book shops for copies of his works since virtually all of his over eighty volumes have been long out of print.[1] His fate has been the classic one of many a man of letters: an auspicious beginning, victorious literary battles, prestigious old age, and surrender to the thickening shades of oblivion.

So severe an eclipse would surely have surprised his later contemporaries. When Shelley and Keats were writing the poetry that would make them immortal, they were considered by many readers to be only Hunt's poetic disciples. Later, after years of political and esthetic warfare were over, Hunt became almost universally accepted as the patriarch of English letters. So irritable and temperamentally different an author as Carlyle regarded Hunt as a genuine, if eccentric genius; and, along with others, Carlyle celebrated the 1850 publication of Hunt's *Autobiography* by declaring it to be "by far the best book of the autobiographic kind" he ever remembered reading in English.[2] Charles Kent, for twenty-five years the editor of the *Times*, thought the book justified "its right to be placed upon the same shelf with Lockhart's Scott, and even with Boswell's Johnson."[3] Even today the book is usually considered a major and characteristic work of the century, and conventional estimates of its author place him after Lamb and Hazlitt as one of the

17

Romantic period's three greatest essayists. Moreover, his well-known essay prefacing *Imagination and Fancy*—an anthology that retained its power to influence readers of poetry until World War I—is considered a sort of common denominator of the Romantic esthetic, and represents Hunt's extensive contributions to nineteenth century criticism. Yet, except for specialists who are usually in pursuit of larger game, very little evidence exists that Hunt is much read presently.

Several reasons for his dramatically diminished reputation are apparent. The inherent limitations of his talent, though genuine enough, were greater than his contemporaries realized. Coupled with this fact was a love of all the verbal arts, which led him to spread his modest talents too thin. He produced a large body of poetry, many excellent translations, an incalculable amount and variety of prose, several plays, and even a three volume novel. Considering the tremendous bulk of his work, a great deal of it has merit; but, had his literary talents and ambitions been more sharply focused, his chances of success would probably have been greater. Another explanation for the reduction of his reputation has been the loss of prestige formerly held by the essay—the form in which Hunt achieved his greatest success but, ironically, the genre least appreciated by present readers. Moreover, as a professional writer, Hunt was forced to invest much of his creative energy in the sort of perishable journalism that, even when available in collected form, possesses too little permanent interest to recommend itself to the reader who does retain a taste for the essay.

Two other somewhat different reasons for his eclipse are also evident. Because of his close literary and personal associations with the great writers of his day he is continually in someone's shadow. Too often only his personal contact and therefore his historical interest concern modern critics; and, as a result, their treatment of his own work is sketchy and condescending. But, even when Hunt is viewed directly, he rarely fares better, because today's critics discover in him little of that temper we call "modern" and that we tend to emphasize in past writers in order to rescue them from the charge of an irrelevant sensibility. We cannot discuss the "disappearance of God" or the "existential dilemma" in a writer whose innocent theology and cheerful esthetics allow no ingenious comparisons with Sören Kierkegaard or Albert Camus. Hunt was a child of the sunlit side of Romanticism; and, though he lived to see the darkness grow and the apocalypse denied, his simple Humanism remained unshaken.

Hunt lived near the center of an unusually rich period of creative activity; moreover, in several modest ways he helped to shape and define that creativity. In addition, he produced works that, while never intended nor capable of bearing up under direct comparison with those of the greatest authors of the day, are still capable of providing their own modest interest and pleasure. The following chapters are intended to suggest something of Hunt's blended historical and intrinsic significance.

## II  *Life*

The best accounts of Leigh Hunt's life are to be found in his *Autobiography* and in Edmund Blunden's excellent biography,[4] and his life is important as a background against which to examine his literary career. When Hunt was born near London in Southgate, Middlesex, October 19, 1784, neither of his parents was a native Britisher. His father, descended from a long line of Barbados churchmen, had been educated in Philadelphia and had practiced law, but his Loyalist sympathies had caused him to flee during the American Revolution. In England, Isaac Hunt, who had taken religious orders, became for a time a popular preacher. Preferment was denied him, however; for, though he had friends and patrons, his bohemian temperament, his lack of diplomatic tact, and, ironically, his liberal politics prevented his advancement. In addition, his even more markedly liberal religious views—he and his Quaker wife became first Unitarians and then Universalists—and his financial irresponsibility helped forestall his worldly success.

These traits and sentiments were to some degree reproduced in his youngest son Leigh, as were his mother's "love of nature and of books."[5] From Mary Hunt, whose shipowner father had entertained Benjamin Franklin and Thomas Paine in his Philadelphia home, Leigh also inherited a taste for music and a strong dread of violence. Hunt was convinced that his mother's saddened and pensive nature had transmitted a degree of timidity to him. Certainly she had enough to make her unhappy; she had surrendered a substantial beginning in life to immigrate; and, when Isaac's new career failed to materialize, he and Mary became familiar with poverty and even debtor's prison. Nonetheless, Hunt's father's good

humor and unshakable cheerfulness provided Hunt with his own
primary characteristic; and his parents' warm interest in politics,
religion, and letters became his interest too.

In 1791, Hunt entered Christ's Hospital School; and he remained
until 1799. This remarkable institution was technically a London
charity school; but, as in Hunt's case, not all of its students were
charity boys. Many of its graduates achieved some fame; but the
best known are Samuel Taylor Coleridge and Charles Lamb, who
preceded Hunt. Like them, he discovered a curriculum that encouraged wide reading, careful, if traditional, writing, and a love of
Classical literature and languages—in short, a most useful basis for
the self-education which Hunt pursued the rest of his life. Two
years before Hunt left school, his affectionate father published
Leigh's early and highly derivative poetry; and, despite its un-
distinguished quality, *Juvenilia* (1801) went through four editions
by 1804 and encouraged Byron to publish his own youthful efforts.
Although the vanity this published work encouraged soon dis-
appeared, Hunt was now unswervingly committed to a life of
letters. After Hunt left school, he assisted in his brother Stephen's
law office for a short time and served as a clerk in the War Office
from 1805 to 1808; however, any potential nonliterary career dis-
appeared when he and his brother John established the weekly *Examiner* in 1808. Throughout his long and active lifetime, Hunt was
to initiate, edit, and write for many journals. But the vigorous
period from 1808 to 1821 gave Hunt the title "Examiner Hunt";
and his work, as Herford says, places him with Hazlitt in 1820
"among the best-hated men in England."[6] Hunt's older brother
John, one of those men who combined liberalism with a sturdy
practicality, had journalistic experience as publisher of the *News*.
The twenty-four year old Leigh had previously written some *Spectator* style essays in the *Traveller* and had provided the theatrical
reviews for John's *News*.

Hunt's was not an auspicious beginning; but he had virtually in-
vented the objective theatrical review; and he now proposed that
the same degree of journalistic impartiality be applied to contemporary politics. Although the *Examiner* was the mouthpiece for no
party, it developed before very long into the chief spokesman for
liberal reform in a nation in full reaction to post - French Revolution and Napoleonic fears. Hunt's political papers matured rapidly
and soon caught the attention of such militant young men as Byron

and Shelley. His fearless attacks on the government brought a series of unsuccessful prosecutions; however, in 1812 his high-spirited but reckless "fat Adonis of fifty" paper on the Prince Regent resulted in a two year imprisonment and in heavy fines for both brothers.

The vivacious young journalist was permitted to share his imprisonment in Horsemonger Lane Gaol with his family—he had married Marianne Kent in 1809 on the strength of the *Examiner's* initial success, and they had their third child in prison—and he converted the grim rooms assigned them into a charming fantasy world of paper rose trellises, book cases, and plaster busts. Old and new friends, including the Lambs, Byron, Hazlitt, Thomas Moore, Jeremy Bentham, and Maria Edgeworth, came to visit or dine in these soon famous quarters with him whom Byron called "the wit in the dungeon." Hunt was always excellent company, and visiting him had the added adventure of observing his extraordinary surroundings.

Such an unusual incarceration has led many an observer to mock its significance and to ignore its impact on Hunt's life. But although Hunt was solvent when he entered jail, he was left in deep financial difficulty as a result of the heavy fines; and, partly because of his temperament, he never really escaped from this financial morass. In addition, his confinement contributed to the deterioration of his health; for, prior to Hunt's imprisonment, his physician had warned him that physical activity such as riding would be necessary if he were to improve. But more important were the psychological effects. In the early weeks of his term, he was never out of earshot of clanking prisoners' chains. Worse, he occasionally observed a gallows being assembled outside his window; and he once witnessed a scene worthy of the creativity of Thomas Hardy that Hunt was never to forget. His jailer, obviously not classing Hunt among the usual prison types, one day took him ostensibly to see the view from the roof; but he actually showed him an attractive young country girl who, awaiting execution for murder of her bastard child, sat trancelike in her cell, "a little hectic spot in either cheek, the effect of some gnawing emotion."[7]

Hunt's two years in prison led to some obvious changes. He loathed the traditional concept of innate evil, and argued instead a theory of social determinism. Moreover, interior decoration could not disguise his own lack of freedom; and, although his rooms were charming, he was a prisoner who held liberty as dear as any man

could. In the summer of 1814, when his family had temporarily left
him, he was ready to dash his "head against the wall at not being
able to follow them."[8] But, when he was at last released on
February 3, 1815, the paradoxical aspect of imprisonment came
home to him; and he realized both the anxiety of freedom and the
deeper sense in which life itself holds us prisoner: "An illness of
long standing, which required very different treatment, had by this
time been burnt in upon me by the iron that enters into the soul of
the captive, wrap it in flowers as he may; and I am ashamed to say,
that after stopping a little at the house of my friend Alsager, I had
not the courage to continue looking at the shoals of people passing
to and fro, as the coach drove up the strand. The whole business of
life seemed a hideous impertinence."[9] He was, therefore, not so
much forced to put down his political pen when he reduced his
production of political articles; rather, he seemed to lose interest in
it or was distracted from it.

Although the *Examiner* continued its opposition to the
state—Hunt had, in fact, carried on his editorial duties while in
prison—following his release Hunt was increasingly spasmodic in his
political involvement. With some improvement in the government,
he was able to turn with a clear conscience to other, less controversial issues. He now devoted more time to poetry; and from this
period came his most ambitious poem, the long romance, *The Story
of Rimini* (1816). But from his release on, it was absolutely
necessary for him to recognize the professional writer's profit
motive. The essentially literary orientation of such journals as his
characteristic *Indicator* (1819 - 1821) represents the marriage of his
natural inclinations with a realization of a new market opened by
growing middle class literacy and by the cultural hunger that such
literacy produced. His liberal political views remained largely un-
changed; he never grew shy of expressing them, but his involvement in direct combat had ceased.

In 1816, Hunt met Keats and renewed an earlier acquaintance
with Shelley. The two young and unrecognized poets (Keats was as
yet virtually unpublished) were drawn to him as his country's
foremost liberal journalist and as a successful, popular poet. For his
part, Hunt responded warmly and immediately to both men. In
Shelley, he perhaps saw what he once might have wished to
become: an idealistic, intense, gifted young poet whose desire for
civil liberty surpassed even his own. By printing Shelley's "Hymn to

Intellectual Beauty" in the *Examiner*, he performed an act of recognition. The powerful friendship that sprang up between the two men was to be, so far as Hunt was concerned, the chief blessing of his life. Hunt's relationship with Keats, while also warm and based on an admiration for a poet able to produce a world of "Flora, and old Pan" more lovely than his own, was more subject to hazard. At the onset of Keats' fatal illness, the relationship ended in misunderstanding and, on Keats' part, some rancor; however, Hunt spent the rest of his life fighting to build that poet's reputation. Late in 1816, Shelley and Keats first met at Hunt's Hampstead lodgings; and, in December, Hunt linked the two poets (along with the now forgotten John Hamilton Reynolds) in his famous "Young Poets" essay in the *Examiner*. Keats, always wary of the influence of others, was not so receptive to Shelley as Shelley was to him. It is symbolic, however, of the powerful association of these three that, when Shelley's drowned body was washed ashore at the Gulf of Spezzia, it was Hunt's copy of Keats' *Lamia and Other Poems* that was found open and folded in Shelley's pocket where it had apparently been thrust in the last minutes of his life.

After an abortive start for Italy in late 1821, Hunt and his growing family finally sailed in the spring of 1822; for the Shelleys had repeatedly urged their coming. Byron and Shelley, having conceived the plan for a new journal to act as a counterblast to Tory periodicals, wished Hunt to join them and contribute his editorial skills; but Shelley had the additionally generous motive of wishing to improve Hunt's chronic bad health. For Hunt, the plan held out new hope; ill and in debt, he had much to gain from the trip, not the least of which was a reunion with his beloved Shelley. His friend's tragic drowning just days after Hunt's arrival was the second major setback in his life, for he was now dependent on the care and wavering good wishes of the changeable Byron. Though they had once been friends, their relationship soon crumbled; and, after four brilliant issues of the *Liberal*, the new partnership dissolved. Byron, all but abandoning the destitute Hunt, left Italy for his fateful role in the Greek Revolution. The Hunts did not return to England until 1825; and, although Hunt loved Italy and admired its literature all his life, his years of insecurity and financially produced exile made an impact on his life similar to that of his earlier imprisonment.

The chief legacy of Hunt's Italian stay, aside from the personal pain caused by the loss of Shelley, was the ill-advised *Lord Byron and Some of his Contemporaries* (1828), written to fill his obligations to a publisher who was then exploiting the Byron legend. On the surface, Hunt's book was well intentioned; but, subconsciously, Hunt's work was an act of revenge against the man who had first humiliated and then cast him aside. Always a target for the most vituperative of conservative reviewers, Hunt's publication brought untold abuse because he had not joined in the wave of elegiac adulation for Europe's most famous modern poet. Earlier attacks on Hunt as the "Cockney King" of literature—as the leader of the "Cockney School," which included Keats and Hazlitt among others—were even more vigorously renewed. Shelley, Keats, and Byron, the principal men of genius whom he had loved or with whom he had been intimate, were dead; and his own reputation was severely diminished.

Yet with such periodicals as the *Tatler* (1830 - 1832), *Leigh Hunt's London Journal* (1834 - 1835), and his *Poetical Works* (1832), Hunt maintained a precarious financial existence and gradually outlived or won over his old enemies. In 1840, his play *A Legend of Florence* achieved a modest success at Covent Garden; and, in 1844, he brought out his popular *Imagination and Fancy*, a poetry anthology important for its theoretical preface and its illustration of Romantic tastes. In the same year, he received a small pension from Sir Percy Shelley, his late friend's son; and the government, once his opponent and persecutor, granted him in 1847 a Civil List pension.

Although the last fifteen years of Hunt's life were easier, they were only relatively so. Marianne died in 1857, ending a long and silently endured trial for Hunt, who had quietly accepted the much decayed sensibility of her later years. He wrote as continuously as ever, producing volume after volume and contributing to most of the leading journals of the day. Perhaps his sheer endurance and continued vitality won him acceptance; for, when Wordsworth died in 1850, Hunt was best known among the remaining old Romantic campaigners. His *Autobiography*, published in the same year, gives us the record of a long past literary warfare; but its genial tone indicates not only his kind nature but also his satisfaction at having survived. He was now the dean of English letters, a venerable, white-haired, handsome old man who was respected by the English and who was sought by such traveling dignitaries as Nathaniel Hawthorne. Charles Dickens' unfair caricature of Hunt as the unscrupulous and insolvent Skimpole in *Bleak House* (1852 - 1853) marred the last decade of his life; but Hunt, more hurt than angry, demonstrated his typical generosity and suppressed his desire for revenge.

When obituaries appeared about Hunt's death at Putney in August 1859, many members of the general public may have been surprised to learn that he had been so recently alive. The famous of his generation were all dead, and Hunt had remained behind to mourn and honor them. Nearly his last essay, for instance, was another in his long defense of Shelley, who had been dead for thirty-seven years. Two men who attended Hunt's funeral remembered the Romantic sunshine that had warmed England in the early nineteenth century. Present was the artist Joseph Severn, whose memory has been perpetuated not by his art but by his attendance upon the dying Keats in Italy. And the adventurer companion of Byron, Edward Trelawney, who shared Hunt's love for Shelley and who had been with him on the beach that scorching day when Shelley's body was cremated, came as well. Hunt's oldest son Thornton, who, like his father, was a journalist and an editor, published the second edition of the *Autobiography* the following year, and a two volume edition of Hunt's letters in 1862. Not until 1869 was the Kensal Green bust dedicated. Its appropriate inscription, drawn from one of Hunt's most popular poems, "Abou Ben Adhem," would have greatly pleased him: "Write me as one who loves his fellow-men."

CHAPTER 2

# The Poet

COULD Leigh Hunt have chosen any successful career he wished, it would certainly have been that of a poet and most probably as a poet modeled after Edmund Spenser. For poetry was Hunt's first love and his earliest literary ambition. *Juvenilia* (1801), the sadly self-explanatory title of his first published poetry, suggests the earliness of this ambition (Hunt wrote these poems "between the ages of twelve and sixteen") as well as the mild pretensions of its author and his overly enthusiastic father. Although these pretensions did not last very long, Hunt was accused in his day of harboring notions about poetic greatness, and he has often been attacked since then for such unjustified pride. At the end of his friendship with Hunt, Keats—frustrated by the discrepancy between his own poetic accomplishments and his passionate ambition—projected into Hunt the "self-delusion" that he actually felt himself.[1]

By the time of Keats' ironic complaint, however, Hunt had realized his very real poetic limitations and certainly did not suffer from the delusions of poetic merit of which Keats accused him. Unlike Keats (and the Romantic poets, in general), Hunt did not write poems about writing poetry, nor did he rehearse the role of bard in Keats' obsessive fashion. Moreover, the pain Hunt probably experienced as he gradually recognized his own poetic worth was outweighed by what for him was the therapeutic nature of the actual writing of poetry, regardless of its quality; and, in this respect, he was very much of his age: " . . . what I write with the greatest composure is verses . . . it is that I write verses when I most like to write; that I write them slowly, with loving recurrence, and that the musical form is a perpetual solace and refreshment.[2]" Hunt's obvious joy in the self-sufficient act of creation, his pleasure in "making," accounts for his encouragement of Keats and Shelley to join him in sonnet-writing competitions—an activity so often scorned by biographers of these two greater poets.

Moreover, Hunt's delight in the activity of writing poetry allowed him to recognize its many possibilities. In the preface to his 1832 volume of collected poems, he confesses his great "reverence" for the art and admits that he "should not dare to apply the term to anything written by me in verse, were I not fortunate enough to be of opinion, that poetry, like the trees and flowers, is not of one class only . . . ."[3] If poetry "in its highest sense" is the property of poets the stature of Shakespeare, he argues, it is in more general terms the "flower of any kind of experience" that springs out of a "real impulse."[4] Not surprisingly, therefore, Hunt vigorously applied the Romantic critical doctrine of sincerity.

Although he was poetically active all his life, with several important exceptions—notably *Captain Sword and Captain Pen* (1835)—Hunt's most interesting poetry was written between 1810 and 1820.[5] In the wide range of poetic genres found in Hunt's works, we see something of the Romantic compulsion toward experimentation (although little of the Romantic power to modify older forms to meet the demands of new experience) and something, too, of Hunt's esthetic instability. Romance, satire, narrative, poetic drama, meditative forms, epistle, sonnets, and other short lyric types—Hunt employs them all. His experimentation is like that of Keats, but it lacks Keats' rapid consolidation. Although Hunt is naturally more successful in some forms than in others, he perfects nothing; and he vigorously develops no potential. Generally, his range is narrower in tone than in form; for his is the poetry of "cheerfulness," which he asserts without embarrassment in his 1818 preface to *Foliage*. With his original poetry as with his translations, his tendency (though not without exceptions) is toward the lighter, gentler, more optimistic.

Henry David Thoreau, voicing a Romantic assumption, argued that "poetry is a piece of very private history, which unostentatiously lets us into the secret of a man's life."[6] In literal terms, Hunt's poetry fails by this definition; we find such self-revelation more often in his essays. But, in a more indirect sense, Thoreau's definition applies; for, although Hunt was forced to be a professional prose writer, his poetry carried him from journalism to a pleasure not otherwise available to him. In prison, he chose to live not as a political martyr but as an esthetic recluse surrounded by a fictional world—one in which he deliberately confused appearance and reality. This same kind of retreat marks much of his poetry; the self-indulgent metrics and imagery, the voluptuousness, and the Romance orientation of much of his nonsatiric poetry expose an undeniably escapist character. Yet, in this escapism, he shares a Romantic tendency.

The chief poetic influences on Hunt are neither complex nor surprising. As a school boy at Christ's Hospital, he had collected the popular Cooke's editions of *British Poets;* and had fallen "passionately in love with Collins and Gray."[7] Thompson was of course a favorite, as was Pope, initially. From the beginning, Spenser was Hunt's special poet; but Hunt had to develop his appreciation of John Milton whose *Paradise Lost* impressed the boy more with its illustrations than with its verse. He learned sufficient Latin and Greek to open the seminal influence of the Classics; and, during his school days, he also read avidly in three books now dull to our eyes: Andrew Tooke's *The Pantheon,* John Lempriere's *Classical Dictionary,* and Joseph Spence's *Polymetis.* With others of his generation, Hunt early developed a love for Italian poetry; and he purchased during his prison stay a set of the *Parnaso Italiano,* which began his long and affectionate study of an Italian literature, that not only influenced his poetic style and attitudes considerably but also produced some of his happiest translations.

The impact of Hunt's great English contemporaries is more difficult to assess. He was slow to recognize Wordsworth, and his opinion of him continually fluctuated. By 1818, he recognized as one of the "properites of poetry" a "sensitiveness to the beauty of the external world";[8] but this view was a general inheritance rather than a specific debt, and little in his work reminds us of Wordsworth. He eventually came to view Samuel Taylor Coleridge as the preeminent poet of the age; but, during Hunt's own period of greatest activity, he was less obviously impressed. Of the second generation poets, Shelley seems to have had some impact on Hunt's later work; with Byron, however, and to a slightly greater degree, Keats, such influence as existed ran briefly in the opposite direction. As we have observed, Byron credited Hunt's *Juvenilia* with nerving him for the publication of his *Hours of Idleness;* Keats' initial imitations of Hunt are well known. Yet if specific influence on Hunt of other Romantic poets is difficult to find, his work is in a very general way a kind of common denominator of many aspects of contemporary poetry.

Hunt's virtues as a poet are largely akin to his vices. Hazlitt, who applauded Hunt's "light, familiar grace," suggested that his proper world was that of the Cavaliers.[9] The casual ease that this association implies accounts also for Hunt's lack of concentration; he was quick, flexible, and relaxed with his verse; but the price he paid was metrical, imagistic, and structural looseness. Only a man of greater talent could have escaped the effects of his undisciplined nature that was too often satisfied with speed, variety, and the immediate enjoyment of sensuous apprehensions. Above all, the vigorous motion that impels us through his better work was achieved by ignoring the complex demands of unity and proportion; for "music," not the total effect, pleased him. His preoccupation with the single line produces some admirable examples; for example, we have the brilliant capsule portrait of Cleopatra as "The laughing queen that caught the world's great hands."[10] Unfortunately, really taut lines like this one are all too rare; for his self-indulgence frequently results in either sudden flatness or cloying luxury. Finally, Hunt's limited vision is conveyed in his poems; the depth or the originality of his insight seldom distracts us from his weakness.

Hunt achieved a justified popularity in his own era; and, despite the biased and often brutal attacks made on him by the critical establishment, he had a solid if modest reputation in the Victorian period. We do not find it difficult to understand why these later readers valued Hunt; he was pleasant, philosophically "cheerful," and comfortably familiar. Perhaps, too, as in "The Nymphs" and in *Rimini,* he managed to be not only mildly titilating but also chaste. Modern readers, however, may recognize the importance of his metrical innovation; but they usually appear unsympathetic to his unpretentious motives and limited successes.[11] Critics and literary historians generally have little patience with the minor artist who has the misfortune to be considered in the company of his creative superiors.[12] Critics who are intrigued by the most famous succumb easily to the temptation to dismiss Hunt's poetry with a pert or, at best, condescending remark—a treatment given most writers in Hunt's position. However, not only Hunt's historical significance but his intrinsic value justify closer examination, for poetry, after all, "like the trees and flowers, is not of one class only."

## I  The Story of Rimini

If Hunt made any real attempt to achieve poetic fame, he did so in the much criticized and warmly praised *The Story* of *Rimini.* Written largely while he was in prison during 1813 - 1814, it was encouraged by Byron, who found in it "a substratum of poetry which is a foundation for solid and durable fame."[13] The poem indeed had its vogue; it was printed in various forms at least ten times before Hunt's death and once again in the year immediately following. For years after its publication, Hunt was known as "the author of *Rimini*" to friends and enemies alike. Although Byron admittedly was more often wrong than right in his literary judgments, he shrewdly recognized that Hunt had in *Rimini* "two excellent points in . . . originality and Italianism."[14] Nor was he alone in his praise. The more rigorous critic Hazlitt found "the whole of the third canto . . . as chaste as it is classical."[15] Among others who praised the work were Augusta Leigh, Samuel Rogers, the Lambs, J. M. Frere, and Thomas Moore. Most of Hunt's contemporary detractors were more nearly politically than esthetically motivated; for Hunt was, after all, the editor of the hated *Examiner*. In our time critics have been busy showing how far his poem falls below the quality of his two famous protégés' work, as though their success with Hunt's metrical innovations can be properly appreciated only if Hunt's performance is made to appear as wretched as possible. Interestingly enough, however, even these critics frequently admit to the existence of a certain verve in the poem, to a kind of genuine life that surpasses the galvanic movements of so many contemporary romances.

This lack of dullness is not the result of *Rimini's* narrative power, however. Hunt's use of Dante's famous tale is quite simple. Canto I concerns the arrival at Ravenna of Duke Giovanni of Rimini's entourage, come to take Francesca to a marriage of convenience with a man she has never seen. Canto II reveals that the haughty prince has sent his younger and altogether more appealing brother Paulo to make her the duke's wife in a proxy ceremony. In sad confusion, she plays the loyal daughter, submits to her father's wishes that she accept; and, following the ceremony, goes with the procession to Rimini to meet her aloof husband. In Canto III, a "fatal passion" entraps the honest Francesca and Paulo, the result of her husband's coolness and thorny pride; and their passion culminates in lovemaking and in immediate regrets. In the final canto, their love affair is discovered by the enraged duke; he challenges his brother to mortal combat; but Paulo, after a struggle in which he realizes that he cannot avoid either killing or being killed, runs on his brother's sword so that the latter will not be his murderer. Giovanni, quite overcome, sends the bodies of his brother and of Francesca, who died after hearing of the combat, to Ravenna for a joint burial.

This brief summary is deceptive since it suggests more action than is actually present in the poem's seventeen hundred lines. In fact, such narrative action as exists is spasmodic and usually transitional. Hunt's chief preoccupation is with alternating descriptions of the characters' physical world and their emotional states. He is most comfortable when dealing with situations, and his descriptions evince obvious delight and perhaps relief. The arrival of Paulo at Ravenna, the unhappy bride's journey to her new home, the pleasure grove, the lovers' state of mind upon recognition of their passions engross Hunt and are the source of the poem's vigor.

This descriptive quality is emphasized when we contrast Hunt's poem with Byron's oriental tales. The materials of *Rimini* are potentially Byronic; an especially strong parallel exists with his *Parisina*, with the chief difference that in Byron's story the lover is the son rather than the brother of the betrayed husband; in fact, Hunt took credit for suggesting, through *Rimini*, the self-incriminating sleep talk of the heroine in Byron's poem.[16] But Byron's tales have sweeping action that is drawn from the pace and the force of narration as well as from the mysterious character of the protagonist. Hunt employs a chronological mosaic in which Giovanni, whose flaws produce this "tragedy," lacks any of the somber qualities of Byron's hero-villains; his pride and coldness tell the whole story. His juxtaposition with the other characters, however, provides Hunt with a series of situations to examine.

Long after its publication, Hunt defended *Rimini* "as a true picture, painted after a certain mode" or "after the fashion of painters," in his " 'first manner.' " Moreover, he could "never forget the comfort" he "enjoyed in painting it."[17] The imagery in this statement (and often found elsewhere in his criticism) is not accidental; he had from the first the strongest interest in the plastic arts. Despite his attraction to and use of music as an analogy to poetry, Hunt often reverted to the older view of the poem as "talking picture." And, if he "invested" his story "with too many circumstances of description" and therefore lost Dante's brevity and force, he made no apologies; for he had had the enjoyment of doing so.[18]

What carries us along in *Rimini* is what carried Hunt himself—the entire tableau, marred as it may be. The poem develops like a series of vivid slide projections; the relationship of the individual descriptions is more mosaic than linear, more a matter of juxtaposition than chronological continuity. The most obvious example of this quality is found in the containing envelope provided by the wedding and funeral journeys which are opposed (and yet contain an ironic similarity) in the poem's overall effect. A subtler example of these juxtapositions can be seen in Hunt's description of the dark woods through which the wedding party must pass as it approaches Rimini and of the situation following their arrival. Giovanni is masculine in the sense that Browning's infamous duke of "My Last Duchess" is masculine, and the picture of the forest prepares us for his sexual (though abstract) domination of the gentle girl: "and still the pine, long-haired, and dark, and tall,/In lordly right, predominant o'er all." [19] These clearly phallic implications lead to the canto's gloomy conclusion:

> A hollow trample now,—a fall of chains,—
> The bride has entered;—not a voice remains;—
> Night, and a maiden silence, wrap the plains. [20]

We are not surprised when Canto III opens with the narrator's dread of telling the story of "the fatal passion" that follows; Francesca's original enslavement is painfully complicated by her feelings for Paulo. The ominous woods are replaced by a pleasure grove that is ostensibly a retreat but is ironically a still more destructive trap.

Similar scenic juxtapositions can be found elsewhere in the poem; and, although they are not always so effective, they provide what unity and coherence the poem possesses. Hunt's tentative organizational principle reminds us of the difficulties encountered by other nineteenth century poets in structuring the long poem. The intellectual and the esthetic sanctions of traditional genres had been lost; for, if each poet is unique, then each poem, it follows, must possess a similar individuality. The search for form became a major, though largely unconscious, preoccupation; and we have only to think of Blake's prophecies, Keats' odes, or Byron's *Don Juan* to illustrate this fact. *Rimini*, in a less profound way, reflects a similar experimentation. Moreover, a curious similarity exists between the nonchronological patterning of Wordsworth's *Prelude* and Hunt's "situational" patterning of *Rimini*. In his *Autobiography* also, Hunt employs a more nearly topical rather than chronological pattern.

The poem's descriptive tableau is enlivened by occasional successes, such as "with heaved-out tapestry the windows glow"[21] or the image of Francesca "glistening like a fairwell star."[22] At times, such lines as "burning stars upon a cloth of blue,— / Or purple smearings with a velvet light"[23] or "it shakes its loosening silver in the sun"[24] call Keats to mind, especially the Keats of "Eve of St. Agnes" and "Lamia." It may have been lines like these that caused Moore to write Hunt that many lines of the poem "haunt me like a passion," doubling the compliment with the allusion to Wordsworth's "Tintern Abbey."[25] However, the Keatsian richness is infrequent. Such lines as the one describing the duke's horses when they "dip their warm mouths into the freshening grass"[26] or the line describing the duke himself who "kept no reckoning with his sweets and sours,"[27] demonstrate Hunt's sturdier achievement, an achievement that helps us survive his numerous coquettish lapses.

Unfortunately, we find it a short step from Hunt's successful lines to the bathos of "she had stout notions on the marrying score"[28] or to the notorious "the two divinest things this world has got, / A lovely woman in a rural spot!"[29] In later revisions, Hunt changed the first of these lines completely and modified the couplet;[30] but these lines, which haunted most hostile readers, are not simply unlucky exceptions since the poem exhibits a strong sense of disproportion between the pathos of Dante's star-crossed lovers and a diction that descends at times to banal chatter. However, Hunt was one of those Romantics who, with Wordsworth, waged war against what he considered to be the sterile poetic diction and formal idioms of the previous century; for he advocated a more conversational style in "the language men really use."[31] Shelley, writing Hunt about "Julian and Maddalo" three years after the publication of *Rimini*, also indicates his agreement: "You will find the little piece, I think, in some degree consistent with your own ideas of the manner in which poetry ought to be written. I have employed a certain familiar style of language to express the actual way in which people talk with each other whom education and a certain refinement of sentiment have placed above the use of vulgar idioms."

Shelley then suggests limitations: he finds the familiar style inappropriate for more elevated productions involving "strong passion."[32] Because Hunt failed to recognize his own improper use of "vulgar idioms," or did not understand the limitations Shelley intended, he frequently employs idiomatic and colloquial language

inadequate to meet the tragic or even serious demands of his subject; and, even worse, he seems never to have recognized his failure
of judgment. However, the poem's glaring examples of stylistic in-
appropriateness are merely the surface indications of a deeper
weakness in the poem, its thematic level. In fact, Hunt appears to
employ Dante's story, not to delineate tragic experience but to
titilate through pathos. We find the expected reference to romance
materials: the lovers read together the Launcelot and Guinevere
story just before they surrender to their passion; earlier, Paulo is
compared with both Launcelot and Tristram; and Paulo's squire is
named Tristram. At the opening of Canto IV, the narrator (who has
no organic role in the poem) appears at first to argue for the cathartic property of poetry—"the poet's task divine / Of making tears
themselves look up and shine—"[33] but it is soon evident, however,
that his motive is not so elevated: "E'en [tragic] tales like this,
founded on real woe, / From bitter seed to balmy fruitage grow"
and "the song that sweetens it" will always be enjoyed for, apparently, its sentimental indulgence.[34]

A later preface makes a different claim. Hunt, arguing that at last
"the world has become experienced enough to be capable of receiv-
ing its best profit through the medium of pleasurable, instead of
painful, appeals to its reflection," describes the work as a clarifica-
tion of "the first discernible causes of the error that produced the
tragedy."[35] Although the reader may think that Hunt's moral theme
involves the lovers' destruction by a father's selfish expediency, he
states that "No: it is not even that. It is the habit of falsehood which
pervaded society around him, and which therefore enabled and encouraged him to lie for that purpose: in other words, it was the great
social mistake, still the commonest among us. . . ."[36] Such an
assumption does not produce tragedy, and the potential tragic
strength and weakness of the characters are never explored; what
are they after all, "but crushed perfumes, exhaling to the sky?"[37]
The comfortable theme of "from bitter seed to balmy fruitage"
suggests an almost Panglossian optimism, and this optimism is not
justified by the reader's experience; easy tears offer neither solace
nor tragic illumination.

Hunt respected poetry of limited motives such as John Pomfret's
*The Choice;* several of his works in this order are admirable, and we
could argue that *Rimini* was too ambitious for the poet's actual
taste. Both the genre and the technique of juxtaposition offer rich
symbolic and mythic opportunities, opportunities that major

Romantic poets like Keats and Shelley successfully exploit; but Hunt, who was content with the kind of poem that could make a lady cry, felt amply repaid for the hostile attacks on the poem by hearing from Samuel Rogers of a "beautiful woman sitting over my poem in tears."[38]

More important than Hunt's pseudo-Wordsworthian practice with colloquial language is his metrical innovation in *Rimini*. "Pope's smooth but unartistical versification" had early held the young Hunt spellbound,[39] but by 1812 the attack against the master was fairly well launched. In *Feast of the Poets*, Pope is charged with having "spoil'd the ears of the town";[40] and, in his subsequent editions, the poet's notes include a long and surprisingly perceptive essay about metrics. Hunt's objection to what he considered the unvaried and sing-song shackles of Pope's verse sprang from a growing interest in the preeighteenth century couplet, especially in the couplets of Chaucer and Dryden, as well as the influence of certain Italian poets. In 1814, Hunt urged his fellow poets "to bring back the real harmonies of the English heroic, and to restore to it half the true principle of its music,—variety."[41] Hunt wished to see not only the pause softened and more often shifted in the line, but also the end stopping reduced as much as possible. This task he set for himself in *Rimini*, but his own success was limited. He "broke up the monotony of Pope," as he was later to claim,[42] for he brought to the form a freedom it had long since lost: he achieved flexibility, ease, and fluidity. But, lacking control, his employment of these qualities rarely produced a line that is not equally marked by a disconcerting slackness.

However, if Hunt's experiment in *Rimini* was largely a failure, he opened a door that was never again shut. Hunt could actually claim that he had had the pleasure "of seeing all the reigning poets, without exception, break up their own heroic couplets into freer modulation (which they never afterwards abandoned). . . ."[43] *Rimini* is therefore of some historical importance: Hunt was a sort of pioneer who opened the way; and, although he could not himself perfect it, he made it available to others. Bate is correct about Keats when he describes him as "imitating not what the master actually did so much as what the master intended to do"[44] since poems like "Lamia" vividly illustrate this fact. Although other poets were interested in Hunt's experiments, Keats is most often associated with his influence. Generally, however, critics have lamented Keats' choice of models and deplored the signs in Keats' work of his ever having read or discussed poetry with Hunt—despite the fact that much of what appears to be the impact of Hunt on Keats' early work was actually the common influence of bad and now forgotten contemporary poetry on both men. Although Keats had, as he himself acknowledged, "something in common with Hunt"[45] only the fairest of Keats' critics admit Hunt's positive contributions to Keats' development: "the enormous benefit Keats derived from Hunt was that Hunt as a model did not inhibit but in fact encouraged fluency. Moreover, he was a model who could in time be surpassed—something, in other words, was left to the powers of the student."[46] In addition to the example of his poetry, Hunt supplied Keats with valuable professional enthusiasm, public exposure in the *Examiner,* and warm personal friendship.

## II   *Mythology and Romance*

The vitality as well as the excesses of *Rimini* can also be found in Hunt's mythological poems of 1818 - 1819—"The Nymphs," "Hero and Leander," and "Bacchus and Ariadne." As in *Rimini,* the narrative development is slight in these works and functions largely as a frame on which to hang descriptive pieces. He delights in Leander's progress through the sea to Hero and in the procession of Bacchus and his enthusiastic entourage toward the abandoned Ariadne; and, for the most part, we delight with him. The abbreviated scope of these three shorter works prevents such cloying properties from overwhelming the reader who prefers dry sherry to sweet port; for Hunt does indulge in the kind of lavish description that, in *Rimini,* Dante's chaste story partially minimizes. These works are characterized by Hunt's version of the luxurious, rich, and sensuous world of Keats' "Flora, and old Pan," which Keats reluctantly admitted in "Sleep and Poetry" he must transcend. The language of "Hero and Leander" is typically voluptuous: trees "tremble" or "pant" and,

> amidst the flush
> Of the thick leaves, there ran a breezy gush;
> And then, from dewy myrtles lately bloomed,
> An odour small, in at the window, fumed.[47]

The waves are "springy," Leander's limbs are "glazy," and "sweetness" pervades everything. In "Bacchus and Ariadne," Bacchus

> Like a ripe world's divinest human flower
> Sat looking forward to the lady's bower.
> Curls trembled in his neck; a crimson vest
> Slung by two clasps, reached half way up his breast.
> His fruity cheek was rounded off, and bent
> Just near the dimpled chin . . . .[48]

Hunt's careless enthusiasm can lead him into such absurdities as his picture of Apollo dancing while " . . . with him danced his hair / In sunny locks."[49] But this same impulse also produces some moderate successes, such as Leander's first meeting with Hero when "the breathless youth / Slid round a gentle cheek, and kissed a warm kind mouth,"[50] or his image of the awakening Ariadne with "her senses lingering in the feel of sleep."[51] Unquestionably, we find a vigorous and often pleasing appreciation of the physical in these poems.

Hunt's considerable taste for these classical subjects does not result in the kind of mythic reinterpretation that so interests us in the works of Keats and Shelley. The meaningful use of existing mythic materials depends upon the artist's ability to redefine them in the terms of his own world. As a critic, Hunt recognized the importance of myth in literature; but, as a poet, he takes no part in the immense Romantic task of reconstructing a mythic framework for the new poetry. He was apparently satisfied with simple restatement, trusting the intrinsic significance and attractiveness to be sufficient. This significance was for him, as Bush points out, "more esthetic and sensuous . . . than religious or mystical."[52]

The most ambitious of these poems, "The Nymphs," deserves even less than the other two to be classified as a narrative. Its two parts consist of, first, a descriptive catalogue of the nymphs; second, a description of the clouds that bring their benevolent rain to the narrator's vantage point on a hill. Hunt creates a large and thoroughly romantic canvas, glossy with supernatural flesh;

> lifting her arms to tie
> Her locks into a flowing knot; and she
> That followed her, a smoothdown-arching thigh
> Tapering with tremulous mass internally.
> Others lay partly sunk, as if in bed,
> Showing a white-raised bosom and dark head,
> And dropping out of an arm.[53]

Hunt's sensuous enjoyment is intense, but his sublimation is quite complete since the truly erotic possibilities never materialize. The nymphs remain nymphs. Opening "The Nymphs" with a traditional appeal to the muses, Hunt begs not for inspiration—"For a new smiling sense has shot down through me, / And from the clouds, like stars, bright eyes are beckoning to me"[54]—but for a translation into the appropriate sylvan location. His muse is "frank, and quick-dimpled to all social glee,"[55] Hunt tells us with perhaps greater perception than he knew; and we are reminded of Keats' acute description of Hunt as "he . . . of the social smile" in his sonnet "Great Spirits Now on the Earth are Sojourning." Certainly, the pleasure principle dominates the poem's spirit; and, at the descriptive center of "The Nymphs" (and on the high altar of his imagination) is the reference that is implied if not stated in much of his other work to the "hoped age of gold."[56] For Hunt, the age of gold is clearly a pastoral one; and Bush accurately says of "The Nymphs" that "nowhere else does Hunt express so poetically . . . his sensitive joy in all the bright and happy phenomena of nature, his loving observation of wood and field and stream and sky, and, one may add, the female form."[57] This deep appreciation results in such fine Keatsian lines as the one describing a moving storm cloud "sloping its dusky ladders of thick rain."[58]

In general, Hunt's nature is more literary and mythic than actual. Poets are as much the normal inhabitants of his landscapes as are flowers and trees, but even more native are those mythological beings most attractive to him, such as the sweet female spirits of Keats' "Flora, and old Pan." Hunt writes as a city man ("I would have the most rural nooks / Just near enough to town to make use of books"[59]) and as an artist. A contemporary, noting his enthusiasm, accurately described his position: "His nature, however, is seldom moor-land and mountain-land; nor is it, for the most part, English nature—we have hints of fauns and the nymphs lying hidden in the shadow of the old Italian woods; and the sky overhead is several tints too blue for home experiences. It is nature, not by tradition, like Pope's nature, nor quite by sensation and reflection, like Wordworth's: it is nature by memory and phantasy; true, but touched with an erotic purple."[60]

Despite "The Nymphs" lack, Hunt occasionally shares Wordsworth's habit of intermingling man and nature in a relationship that is suggestive of some greater, even cosmic, harmony. The opening of *Rimini* and the sonnet "Description of Hampstead" especially call to mind the beginning lines of Wordsworth's "Tintern Abbey," but the difference between the two poets is that Wordsworth brings human life under the influence of nature, and Hunt seems to domesticate the natural world and to convert the whole scene to a still life hung on his study wall. Nonetheless, Hunt's variety of the natural world has in "The Nymphs" (and often elsewhere) its own genuine charm, and his treatment of it is perhaps more typical of the Romantic period than that of Wordsworth himself. Shelley was considerably impressed by "The Nymphs" (despite his annoyance with the Huntian "glib"), and among modern Romantic scholars Douglas Bush thinks the poem to have been possibly Hunt's best.[61] It is interesting as an example of a Romantic vogue and as Hunt's closest point of poetic contact with Keats, as well as for its intrinsic, if limited, merit.

Just as Hunt left no literary genre untried, he attempted the most popular subjects. Since Medieval romance materials had for him an attraction similar to that of mythological narratives, he modernized several Medieval poems;[62] and of his more original poems in this category *The Palfrey* deserves notice. Earlier, he had written "The Gentle Armour," a sometimes sprightly treatment of a young knight's obligation to fight an unwanted battle and of his heroic performance armed only in his lover's shift. The story is literally about "when knighthood was in flow'r," but Hunt chose to employ a tone so light that the poem at times enters the world of farce: the knight was "brave of course, / He stuck as firmly to his friend as horse."[63] Hunt, uncertain of his approach, allows the poem to pass from this modest humor to conventional seriousness, destroying the potentially successful comic tone.

*The Palfrey* (1842), a considerably longer poem than "The Gentle Armour," more consistently explores the same vein. In it, the seriofacetious qualities of the earlier poem are successfully employed in what amounts to a delightful Victorianization of his *fabliau* source. The poem's villains are "those foul old men," an uncle and a potential father-in-law, who, hoarding life as they do their gold, attempt to cheat a young couple of their love by marrying the girl to the young man's miserly uncle. Like an ancient comedy team, the two old men meet to arrange the affair:

> Sir Grey and Sir Guy, like proper old boys,
> Have met, with a world of coughing and noise;
>
> . . .
>
> Now give her to me, I'll give her my gold,
> And I'll give to yourself my wood and my wold.

> And come and live here, and we'll house together,
> And laugh o'er our cups at the winter weather.
>
>                    'A bargain! a bargain' cried old Sir Guy,
>      With a stone at his heart, and the land in his eye.[64]

Hunt's tale contains the usual stuff of such stories; the ending is at once foreseeable, but we find such pleasure in the witty scenes that we quickly read the nine hundred lines of the poem. In fact, the climactic scene is delightful; for, as the would-be marriage procession of fifteen old gray beards conducts the unwilling bride through the night to her new home, the men, armed against the damp air with extra clothing and liquor, fall asleep over their bridles. Their captive female, riding an extraordinary palfrey taken by fraud from her lover, is carried by the clever horse to her lover's arms. Meanwhile, "those owlish men" are carried on by horses who have better sense than they do:

>                                        safe go they,
>      Their drowsy noses drooped away
>      To meet the beard's attractive nest,
>      Pushed upwards from the muffled breast.[65]

And so "the doting set" obliviously ride back to the stables of the old man who had ironically cheated himself out of the girl by employing men still more aged than himself. Royal goodwill is invoked by the young man's influential aunt, the old men are vanquished with scorn, and both conveniently die not long afterward and add their hoards to the king's generosity.

Hunt's continual search for clever variety in portraying obnoxious old age is largely successful, as is his evocation of that archtypal world of comedy where the inevitable conflict between the idealized vitality of youth and the negative qualities of old age can be concluded in only one way. Although we find in his tale neither Chaucerian earthiness nor Byronic wit, Hunt's transformation of the *fabliau* is not a process of emasculation. What emerges from his application of the genre is a sunny romantic world that is enlivened by a rich though restrained humor. It may be worth noting that when *The Palfrey* was published, Victoria was already five years into her reign.

### III   *Satire and* Captain Sword and Captain Pen

An unsigned review of Hunt's satire on William Gifford, "Ultra Crepadarius" (1823), which appeared in his own *Literary Examiner* and which was probably written by Hunt himself, claims two chief justifications for a writer's recourse to satire: "in absolute self-defence; and in a chastisement of the perpetration of vices and follies which have become a public nuisaince."[66] Both excuses were quite orthodox; Pope, for instance, had been motivated by self-defense in his "Epistle to Dr. Arbuthnot," and Dryden had voiced the second argument in his preface to *Absalom and Achitophel.* Hunt rephrased both justifications in his preface to the 1832 edition of his poems but admitted there—as he did again in his *Autobiography*—that neither had been the motive for writing his first major poem, the satire *Feast of the Poets*, published initially in 1811.

This "effusion," as he was later to call this poem,[67] was the subjective and "presumptuous" product of the errors that a young writer is liable to make when he applies his unseasoned judgment to older men. This poem, written at an age when Hunt still regarded "a satire as nothing but a pleasant thing in a book,"[68] had the result, he claimed, of making "almost every living poet and poetaster my enemy."[69] That he came to genuinely regret many aspects of his attack is clear, but for various obscure reasons he did not follow Byron's example in the case of *English Bards and Scotch Reviewers* and suppress this "jeu d'esprit" suggested by the "*Session of the Poets* of Sir John Suckling."[70] Years later, with a mixture of honest confession and pride, he summarized what he felt had been the literary world's reaction:

> I offended all the critics of the old or French school by objecting to the monotony of Pope's versification, and all the critics of the new or German school, by laughing at Wordsworth, with whose writings I was then unacquainted, except through the medium of his deriders. . . . I had not very well pleased Lord Byron himself, by counting him inferior to Wordsworth. Indeed, I offended almost everybody whom I noticed.[71]

The method Hunt employed in the *Feast of Poets* is simple for, as the title suggests, he has Apollo descend for a feast with the chief contemporary poets of England. Many writers present themselves, including those we now consider most significant from that period; but Apollo with varying degrees of scorn and cruelty dismisses most of them and concludes in the first edition with an order for "Laurels four!"—Thomas Campbell, Robert Southey, Sir Walter Scott, and Thomas Moore. We are amused not only by Hunt's want of judgment here (though many contemporary readers would hardly have been shocked), but also by the arrogance of his indictment of Wordsworth who had "been so benurst, / Second childhood with him had come close on the first," and of Coleridge who had troubled Apollo "long since, I suppose. / By his idling, and gabbling and muddling in prose."[72] Of these two now famous poets,

> one began spouting the cream of orations
> In praise of bombarding one's friends and relations;
> And t'other some lines he had made on a straw,
> Showing how he had found it, and what it was for.[73]

Enraged, Apollo shouts his dismissal:

> What! think ye a bard's a mere gossip, who tells
> Of the ev'ry-day feelings of everyone else,
> And that poetry lies, not in something select,
> But in gathering the refuse that others reject?
> Depart and be modest, ye driv'llers of pen,
> My feasts are for masculine taste, and for men.[74]

There are other such critical indiscretions and not a few justifiable shots at a host of minor poets and playwrights. The weak state of poetic art stems, it appears, from the "reason and rhyme"[75] that followed the passing of two poets Hunt deeply admired, Milton and Dryden:

> ever since Pope spoiled the ears of the town
> With his cuckoo-song verses, one up and one down,
> There has been such a whining or prosing . . .[76]

This critical bias against what he called the "French School"[77] was at the root of the metrical innovations we observed in *Rimini*.

The quality of the just quoted passages demonstrates that on stylistic grounds, too, the poem leaves much to be desired. Yet, rather than withdraw the poem, Hunt published it several more times during the years; and each time he made numerous alterations and added additional notes. Originally included in his *Reflector,* it was published separately in 1814, again in 1815, and reprinted in the collected editions of 1832, 1844, and 1860. The progress of these revisions and the ever more copious notes that accompany them form a record of Hunt's growing critical maturity and changing taste. They allow us to trace the rise of Wordsworth and Coleridge in Hunt's favor, the admission of Byron to the feast, and in later editions the inclusion of Keats and Shelley, among others. However, the exciting audacity of the original is lost; and the notes to these editions, rich in the critical controversy of Romanticism, retain the greatest interest.

Hunt's other satires about literary subjects are no more successful. "The Book of Beginnings" is notable only for Hunt's adoption of the otava rima of Byron's *Don Juan.* "Ultra-Crepadarius," which, like "The Book of Beginnings," was published in the *Liberal* in 1823, is an attack on William Gifford, a satirist and the unattractive editor of John Murray's *Quarterly Review.* Hunt fails in this piece largely because he does exactly what he attacks Gifford in *The Feast of the Poets* for doing: smashing an insect with a heavy club. Introduced as a companion satire to *Feast, Blue Stocking Revels* (1837), has, in fact, little of the satirical about it. In the course of a long alphabetical catalogue of now mostly forgotten female authors (many of whom Hunt admits not having read), a few glancing shots are fired. There is, for example, the controversial line in which Lady Blessington is seen as "a Grace after dinner! A Venus grown fat!" or the one in which Apollo unencouragingly confesses that Margaret Cullen's chief virtue is to put him to sleep.[78]

But, whereas even the later versions of the *Feast* exclude more than they include, *Blue Stocking* opens the door to every woman of any literary pretensions whatsoever. The tone is gallant, clever, and arch, especially at the poem's climax, where agents of Apollo swoop under the banquet table to apply the sorority's emblem:

> a shriek of sweet wonder
> Rose, sudden and brief, as of fear come and gone;
> And 'twas felt thro' the room, that the stockings were *on!*[79]

Such gentle amusements as this bit of titillation seem more central to Hunt's motives than the sharp satirical treatment this crew largely deserved. We have only to recall Byron's "The Blues" or his

crushing portrait of Lady Byron as Donna Inez in *Don Juan* for
some idea of how the subject might have been handled. But Hunt,
an early champion of woman's equality and always a gentleman
where ladies were concerned, is content with a little gentle chiding
before he concludes by rebaptizing them *"true violets"* and by
reserving blue for "the masculine, vain, and absurd."[80] Though this
satire obviously lacked the fire and critical audacity of the earlier
*Feast*, Hunt was pleased to recall Samuel Rogers' claim that the
piece was sufficient "to set up half a dozen young men about town
in a reputation for wit and fancy."[81]

Hunt's political satires possess greater potential than his typically
diffuse literary attacks, largely because of their more specific subjects and his strong political feelings. But when judging them, we
must remember that, with the possible exception of the slightly
more ambitious "The Dogs" (1822), written for the aggressive
*Liberal*, these poems, like so much of Hunt's prose, are perishable
journalistic exercises, often mere squibs. Since more than half of all
his satires were never reprinted and since others were reprinted only
once, Hunt recognized their slight value.

It is curious, however, that—given his powers of observation,
courage, and political convictions—certain subjects did not move
him to greater effort. His old enemy the Prince Regent, hanging
judges, and well-fed dogs found among starving soldiers—any of
these topics would seem ideal for Hunt's satiric purpose. Yet his
treatment of the regent in "The St. James Phenomenon" (1814) and
in "Coronation Soliloquy" (1821), while not without merit, certainly lacks the vigor and pithiness of the essay that earned him the
prison term. These poems tend to be clumsy ("his brains are
veal, / And his heart of steel, / And his blood rum-punch and
hollands") or simply dispirited ("Bags, Bags, Sherry Derry,
periwigs, and fat lads, / Save us from our wife O!").[82] Hunt's
weakness does not stem from a want of anger at the numerous examples of social injustice around him. In "Reverend Magistracy"
(1819), one of his many "Harry Brown" poems, Hunt describes two
children of poverty arrested for sleeping in a brick kiln. The judge
proclaims their behavior to be a "gross enormity! / What spirited
deformity!" and then goes on to point out that "comfort's no poor
man's business" since "they must be thinned at any rate, / Says
Malthus."[83]

We might expect "The Dogs" (1822), his most ambitious political
satire, to be more devastating. Taking as his starting point a journal

entry of a soldier in the Peninsular Campaign who relates his mixed feelings about having been assigned the duty of breaking biscuits for Wellington's hounds and thereby alleviating his own hunger, Hunt ironically "shows us (never to want proof again) / What very different things are brutes and men":

> The subject will excuse me for my brain:
> To write's but human, but of dogs divine.
> I shamefully forgot, great Sir, that when
> Dogs are considered, what are men?[84]

Here is a subject for Swift, or even for Byron, whose fellowship on the *Liberal* no doubt encouraged Hunt to treat the subject in octava rima, as it had done in the case of "The Book of Beginnings." The poem is a sort of Huntian "Modest Proposal": if dogs are to be treated better than humans, they should also be elevated to the aristocracy and taken into heaven. But, despite another of Hunt's processions (this time the potentially amusing triumphal entry of the dogs), the best he can do is suggest the dogs' superior value because they stimulate the iron duke's spirits: "they, blessed creatures, saved him from ennui."[85] Though only 408 lines, the poem drags out in boredom: Hunt cannot sustain his attack.

Among the Romantics, only Byron chose to carry satire beyond a derivative exercise, to adapt it to the new age; for it was no longer a popular or prestigious genre. Yet the weakness of Hunt's satire results not so much from this esthetic shift of emphasis as from his very nature. Despite his wit and his youthful zeal and enthusiasm, his tolerant, cheerful character largely incapacitated him for literary warfare. Consequently, "in playing with the lighter weapons of much greater wits of old time," as he put it, he worried about doing "an unnecessary thing, calculated to give a wrong kind of pain."[86] Moreover, he seemingly never took satire seriously in its classical or in its cathartic sense.

Linked to the satires by deep ironies and by intense social criticism is one of Hunt's most unusual poems, *Captain Sword and Captain Pen* (1835; and it is unusual because he achieves in this work what was for him a remarkable power and manliness, not only through the communication of strong convictions, but also by the use of heavy and provocative rhythms. "The measure is regular with an irregular aspect,—four accents in a verse,—like that of Christabel, or some of the poems of Sir Walter Scott," Hunt tells us.

He then presents a sample scansion for those new members of the "reading public, whose knowledge of books is not yet equal to their love of them."[87]

Like *Rimini*, *Captain Sword and Captain Pen* is scenic in nature; and Blunden has rightly discussed it in cinematic terms.[88] This passionate indictment of war is divided into six vivid sections. The poem opens with Captain Sword on the march; his army and its trappings delight the hearts of viewers who feel deep "sympathy" for his cause, though ominously "the drums and the music say never a word."[89] The second scene portrays a great victory for Sword—during a battle fought, unhappily for Hunt, in "a spot of rural peace"—and described with considerable vigor:

> Down go bodies, snap burst eyes:
> Trod on the ground are tender cries;
> Brains are dashed against the plashing ears;[90]

It is a "mad-house" grown "liquid with lives," this "fleshiest feast of Death."[91] In the midst of these unflinching descriptions the reader is urged to "shrink not . . . Thy part's in it too; / Has not thy praise made the thing they go through / Shocking to read of, but noble to do?"[92]

The third section, which is brief, describes a victory ball given in honor of Sword; and this scene serves as an appropriate, ironic contrast, not only with the previous battle but, more intensely, with the next section that pictures the battlefield on the following night—the most deliberately horrible scene of the poem. Reflecting man's own spiritual and mental disorder, nature is disturbed, and the "wind is mad upon the moors."[93] Among the torn, dying, and dead move human vultures: "the floor [of 'the Dance of Death'] is alive" with "mute creatures of prey"[94] who are performing an awful parody of ministration. Evidence of brutal slaughter and ensuing misery is everywhere; but, unless such mass destruction appear too abstract, too boggling, the reader is given a representative "but one"—a bridegroom and son who is dying of a saber slash—to individualize the horror. Placed in the center of his description is the poem's primary thesis:

> "I will not read it!" with a start,
> Burning cries some honest heart;
> "I will not read it! Why endure

> Pangs which horror cannot cure?
> Why—oh why? and rob the brave,
> And the bereaved, of all they crave,
> A little hope to gild the grave?"
>
> Asketh thou why, thou honest heart?
> 'Tis *because* thou dost ask, and *because* thou dost start.
> 'Tis because thine own praise and fond outward thought
> Have aided the shows which this sorrow has wrought.[95]

The argument that men condone war if they do not cause it is dramatized several times in the poem. Hunt was convinced that we must reject this passive acceptance, and his unyielding emphasis on war's brutalities is designed to force us into a recognition of, first, what war actually is, and, second, wherein our guilt lies. The section concludes with Hunt's urgent plea and hope: "Oh, God! let me breathe, and look up at thy sky! / Good is as hundreds, evil as one; / Round about goeth the golden sun."[96]

The fifth part of the poem demonstrates how Sword's victories cost him his reason (which Hunt equates with his soul); but this section also makes references to the American Revolution, the French war, Wellington as a kind of Sword, and the rise of Captain Pen. The final section details the nonviolent combat of Pen, who is armed with "only a letter calm and mild,"[97] and Sword, who is weakened by having lost his hold on men's minds. The poem concludes with a version of the Romantic apocalypse, the expression of which links Hunt not only to his friend Shelley but also to Wordsworth and Blake:

> And when Captain Sword got up next morn,
> Lo! a new-faced world was born;
> For not an anger nor pride would it show,
> Nor aught of the loftiness now found low,
> Nor would his own men strike a single blow:
> Not a blow for their old, unconsidering lord
> Would strike the good soldiers of Captain Sword;
> But weaponless all, and wise they stood,
> In the level dawn, and calm brotherly good;
>
> . . .
>
> "O last mighty rhet'ric to charm us to war!
> Look round—what has earth, now it equably speeds
> To do with these foul and calamitous needs?

> Now it equably speeds, and thoughtfully glows,
> And its heart is open, never to close?"[98]

This hopeful conclusion is not achieved without considerable pain for Hunt, who was forced to write the gruesome passages, and for the reader who is compelled to read them. Only "a sense of duty" produced by the threat of renewed European warfare turned Hunt from the less painful subjects he admittedly preferred.[99] Not since the early *Examiner* days had he felt so passionately the need to dramatically alter what he saw as the conventionally passive approbation of man's basic inhumanity to man. He was incensed that even such a "great poet and philosophical thinker" as Wordsworth himself could slip so far as to write of God:

> But thy most dreadful instrument,
> In working out a pure intent,
> Is man, arrayed for mutual slaughter:
> Yea, carnage is thy daughter.[100]

Hunt continued to battle this attitude with new prefaces, lengthy notes, and excerpts from battle memoirs that accumulated greatly as the poem went through various editions. From the outset, his assumption remained the same: "all passionate remedies for evil are themselves evil, and tend to reproduce what they remedy."[101] Since he regards evil as ignorance to be eliminated, not as intrinsic depravity, Hunt created Captain Pen, who represents not just journalism but the combined cultural and educational powers of all fields of writing.

Although *Captain Sword* is intended to be didactic, Hunt neither in practice nor in theory openly advocated didactic literature. As such, *Captain Sword* reminds us more of Shelley's *Mask of Anarchy* (which Hunt had published three years earlier) than of Blake's *French Revolution,* or of other still more exotic and mythic Romantic treatments of the social millenium. Hunt's poem shares something of the "more or less everyday language" employed by Shelley in hopes of moving a large and varied audience.[102]

## IV   "Mild Singing Clothes"

Hunt discovered, but failed as usual to exploit, a potentially more successful mode in which to realize his version of the Golden Age than he had found in the materials of romance. Contemplating John

Pomfret's *The Choice* (1700), a poem voicing the suburban longings of urban man that are found so frequently in Western poetry, Hunt felt a sympathetic bond and was moved to write his own version in "The Choice" (1823) which consists of a description of the rural retreat where Hunt would find all the joys that he desires: a kind of domesticated nature, a modest home for his friends, the usual book-lined study, and the proper sort of wife.

But more than Pomfret's theme appealed to Hunt, who saw Pomfret's work as "a pretty kind of—sort of—kind of thing, / Not much a verse, and poem none at all." He admired the poem for being "extremely natural" but not simply for that quality: "And yet I know not. There's a skill in pies, / In raising crusts as well as galleries."[103] In Pomfret's modest art, he detected a quality he could warmly appreciate: " . . . he's the poet, more or less, who knows / The charm that hallows the least thing from prose, / And dresses it in its mild singing clothes."[104] Hunt recognizes that, like Pomfret, he may hope to give joy because, though "the greatest poets please the greatest wits," yet "every reader loves the least by fits."[105] Hunt devised no eminently quotable lines in this poem; its charm lies in its quiet, unpretentious pursuit of an essentially middle class and distinctly Huntian ideal world. Its sentiments are unexceptional; but, by avoiding both the voluptuousness of his romances and the posturing of his satires, he is able to exercise his modest ability.

In the years to come, Hunt wrote several more poems in this humble vein. He chose the more appropriate blank verse for "Thoughts in Bed upon Waking and Rising" (1834), "Our Cottage" (1836), and "A Rustic Walk and Dinner" (1842). "Thoughts in Bed" he subtitled "An 'Indicator' in Verse," an "original *verse essay* written in the spirit of the paper under that name."[106] This note suggests his awareness of the familiar essay quality of these poems, as does his note to "A Rustic Walk and Dinner" which warns the reader that the blank verse is "intentionally unelevated, in accordance with the familiar and colloquial nature of the subject;—it is literally *sermo pedestris*,—poetry on foot."[107] While not without esthetic blunders and while often balanced precariously between sentiment and sentimentality, these poems share with "The Choice" an element of Hunt's slender grace. They are pleasant rather than provocative; there is a quiet good will about them that is carried along by an easy but not vulgar style. His forte was the personal prose essay, a vehicle for sharing with the reader those nice obser-

vations about life, nature, and art that came so easily to him. This
talent gently supports these poems. Whether it leads to a comment
on the simple joy of the day's return when

> the white window shows
> Difference from darkness, and the world goes round
> In order, safe within the force of God,
> And gentle light is sweet for its own sake[108]

or to giving voice to the traditional English love of rural life where
"farms are all men's homes, / A sort of homely golden age in fancy,"[109] Hunt's mild sentiments generally please. Here again we find
Keats' Hunt "of the social smile," and it is unfortunate that he did
not practice more extensively in this limited form.

### V  Sonnets and Other Lyrics

Hunt's forty odd exercises in the Italian sonnet share something
of the quality of these gentle, unpretentious poems. "Quiet
Evenings" with its theme of "tiny hushings" and his six sonnets on
Hampstead Heath especially possess this mood. In general,
however, Hunt's work in this demanding form is unexceptional; for
the principal themes of friendship, the appreciation of a cozy,
domesticated natural world, patriotism, liberty, and art are handled
with a minimum of originality and invention. They are largely occasional poems marking some personal event, association, or temporary enthusiasm. More than half are addressed to, or directly concern, friends or people whom he admired (including Shelley, Keats,
Benjamin Haydon, Charles Dickens, and Thaddeus Kosciusko).
Even the receipt of a lock of Milton's hair produces two sonnets.

Only twice, beyond an occasional line here and there, do these
poems transcend Hunt's personal history. The frequently
anthologized "Grasshopper and the Cricket" (1816), which was
produced in a sonnet-writing competition with Keats, is charming
in its unaffected whimsey:

> Green little vaulter in the sunny grass,
>     Catching your heart up at the feel of June,
>     Sole voice that's heard amidst the lazy noon,
> When ev'n the bees lag at the summoning brass;—
> And you, warm little housekeeper, who class
>     With those who think the candles come too soon,

> Loving the fire, and with your tricksome tune
> Nick the glad silent moments as they pass;—[110]

The pleasant unity of tone and form in this poem is unusual in Hunt's work, but the winner of the competition should be Keats because of his sonnet's fine opening line—"The poetry of earth is never dead."

But in a second sonnet competition (1818) that included Hunt, Keats, and Shelley, Hunt was victorious. The impromptu subject was the Nile, and Hunt's effort produced not only his best sonnet but his finest short poem. Versification and rhetoric are perfectly harmonized in this lovely evocation of the fabled river that flows "through old hushed Egypt and its sand, / Like some grave mighty thought threading a dream."[111] We are reminded, as Blunden aptly suggests, of the "shadowy infinitudes of Blake."[112] The best lines—especially the deservedly well-known description of Cleopatra as "the laughing queen that caught the world's great hands"[113]—are produced by a seriousness that is for once unmarred by either clichés or extravagances. The poem's real subject is eternity, both in the agelessness of the Near East and in the parallel between the Nile's timeless flow and "our own calm journey on for human sake."[114] Had Hunt written poems of this quality more frequently, his modest reputation would have been secure.

In addition to the sonnets, three other widely anthologized short poems should be mentioned here. Two of these, "Abou Ben Adhem" and "Rondeau" (both written in 1838), must be placed in that class of popular poetry so often treated with condescension by critics, despite the fact that its very survival without their praise proves that some intrinsic merit recommends it to our collective appreciation. The appeal of the "Abou Ben Adhem" no doubt lies in its memorable simplicity and in the Blakean thesis that the love of man is actually the love of God. "Rondeau" possesses not only this simplicity but also an even more severe economy. Like most of Hunt's poetry, this poem is a product—to use his own Romantic dichotomy—of fancy rather than imagination, but his use of the personal and at the same time archetypal situation is an unqualified success:

> Jenny kissed me when we met,
>     Jumping from the chair she sat in;
> Time, you thief, who love to get

> Sweets into your list, put that in:
> Say I'm weary, say I'm sad,
>     Say that health and wealth have missed me,
> Say I'm growing old, but add,
>     Jenny kissed me.[115]

The poem's Jenny was Carlyle's delightful wife Jane. Despite the autobiographical base, however, the thematic force stems from genuine sentiment, not bogus sentimentality. Technically, the poem is not a *rondeau;* for Hunt apparently uses the term in the loose sense employed by early English practitioners.

The third of these well-known poems, "The Fish, the Man, and the Spirit" (1840), is actually a dialogue in which the three parts are cast in sonnet form. The first two units initially strike the reader as pleasingly ingenious and as nothing more. The human and the fish points of view are amusingly contrasted; fish are seen as those "astonished-looking, angle-faced, / Dreary-mouthed, gaping wretches of the sea" who are "legless, unloving, infamously chaste."[116] The fish sees man with his "flat and shocking face" as a horrible joke: "with a split body and most ridiculous pace, / Prong after prong, disgracer of all grace."[117] An absolute mystery to each other—"what is't ye do? What life lead?"—the fish can only marvel at this strange, dry land "breather of unbreathable, sword-sharp air."[118]

In the third section, however, when the fish is metamorphized into a man and then into a spirit before speaking again, the poem becomes more nearly metaphysical than simply witty. Playfulness is replaced by a dignified seriousness:

> Man's life is warm, glad, sad, 'twixt loves and graves,
>     Boundless in hope, honoured with pangs austere,
> Heaven-gazing; and his angel-wings he craves:—
>     The fish is swift, small-needing, vague yet clear,
> A cold, sweet, silver life, wrapped in round waves,
>     Quickened with touches of transporting fear.[119]

The speaker, now "a visitor of the rounds of God's sweet skill" probes for and appears to find the necessary difference; and he urges man to "loathe, but with a sort of love; / For difference must its use by difference prove."[120]

## VI  *Masque and Drama*

Because of Hunt's early professional interest in the theater (he was writing reviews by 1805) and his compulsion to try his hand at various literary forms, we are not surprised to discover among his work a masque and several poetic dramas. The theme of the masque, *The Descent of Liberty* (1815), can be seen in his "Ode for the Spring of 1814" that was reprinted as a pendant to the longer work. The ode is an apocalyptic vision of the earth's revival that is combined with man's spiritual and political rejuvenation through liberty and with his delight in the new "green and laughing world" that he sees when his prison walls are destroyed.[121] In the masque's prologue, Liberty promises to "descend in lustre through the freshened air, / Met by the flowering spring" and then "lead a lovelier period for mankind."[122] The long allegorical poem opens before the "Enchanter" (an inappropriate alias for Napoleon) is destroyed by Liberty and before the long celebration of Peace, Music, Painting, and Poetry (followed by other salutory presences) begins. The playing of Prussian, Austrian, Russian, and English marches alerts us to the allegory of the allied victory over Napoleonic France, the poem's historical basis and ostensibly the source of Hunt's strong optimism. But, beyond this general context, the poem's historical dimension is very slight; influenced by the Romantic vision genre, the poem works on a symbolic level and is concerned with the resultant state of cultural grace rather than with the victory itself. Hunt's optimistic view of man's progress manifests itself in a theory of spiral amelioration: "all human good / Mounts by degrees"; but some back sliding is to be expected.[123] And essential to any rapid improvement is Liberty, who for Hunt is God's true daughter, not Wordsworth's "Carnage."

Both Hunt's convictions and the visionary-allegorical form remind us of Shelley and Blake. The former is recalled in the spiritual music that hovers over the masque's opening, as well as in the poem's general sentiments and, at times, language. Blunden sees the speech of Hunt's Sable Genius, for instance, as "one of the loftiest and most Shelleian passages outside of Shelley."[124] Among others, the following lines contain a thought strongly reminiscent of Blake:

> you've heard me, Sir,
> In my young fancy picture out a world,
> Such as our present-timed, unfinal eyes,

> Knowing but what they see,—and not even that,—
> Might gather from the best of what's before them,
> Leaving out evil as a vexing thorn,
> Whose use they know not;—[125]

In short, we have in these passages the Romantic and particularly Blakean doctrine of the limitations of ordinary vision and the implication of the imagination's superiority. The difference between what will be and what the "unfinal eyes" now see reminds us of Blake's argument that a man who possesses fewer than five senses and who is unaware of the others could not deduce their existence without imagination. Other Romantic ideas in this characteristic poem include the millenial dream of a world that is envisioned in the imagery of the resurrection, as "just like a new creation,—Spring and Summer / Married, and Winter dead to be no more."[126]

These dreams of a new world were heartfelt themes for Hunt, who was fantasizing and writing behind the bars of Horsemonger Lane Gaol where his own imprisonment and release in 1815 may have initially seemed a part of the prologue to a great renewal. But such personal investment, real as it is, fails to vitalize *The Descent of Liberty*, which remains interesting largely on extrinsic grounds. The potential of the poem is clear, but such scenes as the fire battle of two hostile clouds, such phrases as "nice-leaved lesser lilies" and "genteel geranium," such lines as "Phaniel, if your cloud holds two, / I'll come up, and sit with you!" turn a variety of serious poetry always susceptible to bathetic plunges and cruel parody into the unintentionally comic.[127] Years later Hunt claimed to see "a vein of something true" in the piece, but he acknowledged the victory of fancy over imagination.[128]

Hunt's revival of the masque, a genre that had been out of fashion for a hundred and seventy-five years, illustrates his enthusiasm for literary experimentation as well as his love of the Renaissance. Equally typical is his long and pleasant preface, "Some Account of the Origin and Nature of Masks," another example of his cultural sharing. In this discussion, Hunt admits that his original plan for the production of *The Descent of Liberty* was abandoned because of technical staging difficulties. He concludes the essay, however, with an interesting discussion of the virtues of closet drama, arguing that, as his masque had been "written partly to indulge the imagination," it was in "the liveliness of their own apprehensions" that readers could best enjoy his work. "Who, that has any fancy at all," he asks, "does not feel that he can raise much better pictures in his own mind than he finds in the theatre?"[129] Blunden suggests that this statement indicates the gulf between the "temporary" and "physical" observations of Hunt and the "permanent" and "metaphysical" judgments of Lamb.[130] Yet Hunt's claim is remarkably similar to Byron's plea for a "mental theatre." Despite their rationalization, their attitude represents the dimly emerging awareness of the failure of the old drama in the post-Enlightenment world, an awareness that would lead eventually through a wasteland of conventional and experimental drama to a revitalized form.

The thesis that "mental theatre" is somehow superior to the actual stage prevented neither Byron nor Hunt from yielding to the theater; for Hunt produced other, more conventional dramatic attempts, most of which are in verse. Recognizing the worthlessness of his earliest experiments, Hunt neither published nor presumably saved them. Some later attempts (one or two in which Hunt placed great faith) were published; and two, *A Legend of Florence* and "Lovers' Amazements", were performed. Two versions of one play and a second play are extant in manuscript: "The Secret Marriage," "The Prince's Marriage," and "The Double." The first, in Hunt's view, was rejected by the theater because "in these effeminate days of the drama" tragedy "would not be endured;" the second was refused because theatergoers wanted "nothing but sops and honey," and Hunt's play was found insufficiently "pleasant."[131]

The published plays include a dramatic fragment (1820) and three plays: "A Father Avenged" (one act, 1820), *A Legend of Florence* (five acts, 1840), and "Lover's Amazements or, How Will it End?" (three acts, 1851). A previously unpublished fragment and a two act play in prose, "Look to Your Morals," were first published by Milford in 1923. The latter, a sprightly after piece, is mildly attractive; otherwise among the published plays only *A Legend of Florence* retains any substantial interest. This play, though written sometime earlier, was both published and performed in 1840; and it had fifteen or twenty nights at Covent Garden. The play's warm reception encouraged Hunt to hope that here, at last, was his road to fame and much needed financial security.

Hunt had some justification for this unrealized desire; for, when contrasted with most contemporary dramas and even much of Hunt's own work, *A Legend of Florence* displays a marked restraint. The plot is of course silly: Rondinelli still loves Ginevra, whom he had courted before her marriage to the most unpleasant Agolanti. She is faithful to her selfish husband, who nonetheless allows her to seemingly die from an unattended illness. Upon her revival in the tomb, she seeks refuge with Rondinelli and his virtuous mother. When Agolanti learns that she still lives, he comes to claim her and is killed in a scuffle. We conclude that the two lovers will now be properly united, although, prior to her flight, Ginevra's plan had been to enter a convent.

However, the play is less unfortunate in its content than this bare plot summary would make it appear. Symons, a scholar for the most part harshly critical of Hunt's poetry, finds "the gentle Elizabethan manner . . . caught up and revived for a moment" and a "human tenderness which may well remind us of such more masterly work as 'A Woman Killed With Kindness.' "[132] Certainly the blank verse is supple enough to give a fair degree of flexibility to Hunt's dialogue, and little of the histrionics that the plot summary might suggest actually exist. Moreover, considering the unpromising materials, Hunt manages to give the play a sense of wholeness that few of his works possess. In his long analysis of the failure of nineteenth century drama, Nicoll attributes to Hunt's play "a power of construction and an ease of dialogue," firm character outlines, "true life," and "a strength which is wanting elsewhere" in the drama of his age.[133]

But we must conclude that Nicoll is somewhat too generous. An old hand at turning out credible performances, Hunt could get the plot moving and people talking; but he lacked a sense of their dramatic relationship. Contrary to Nicoll's suggestion, it is not his choice of an unrealistic theme[134] that weakens the play; rather, it is his failure to exploit the symbolic resources of that theme in any significant way. Consequently, the result verges at times on theatrical puppetry and ventriloquism; and the "life" of Hunt's work is neither symbolic nor "true"; it is mechanical. Moreover, like other would-be Romantic dramatists, Hunt failed to see the danger of trying to resuscitate a dead tradition. His success as a dramatic critic reminds us again how often he could recognize artistic merit in others but fail to produce it himself.

Though revived at Sadler's Wells in 1850 and given a command performance at Windsor Castle in 1852, A Legend of Florence failed to become one of those oft-repeated successes of the nineteenth century theater. By the time of the uneventful production of his "Lovers' Amazements" at the Lyceum, January 20, 1858, Hunt had long realized his failure as a dramatist.

## VII   *Translations*

Shelley, hearing that Hunt was at work on a translation of Tor-quato Tasso's *Amyntas*, complained to his friend that he should instead be exercising his "fancy in the perpetual creation of [his own] new forms of gentleness and beauty." Although Hunt's translation of the poem almost reconciled him to time spent in that way, Shelley noted that Hunt "might have written another such poem as the 'Nymphs,' with no great access of effort."[135] Were all Hunt's poetic efforts as successful as the section of the poem that Shelley cites, he might have some sort of case. However, the quality of Hunt's translations is often much finer than that of his original creations.

It was Hunt's fidelity to the original that accounts for much of his success as a translator; his method was, he said, to "read closely and with a due sense of what the poet demands."[136] The discipline provided by the original was the control he so badly needed, for it allowed him to avoid the excesses that all too often mar his own work. We may compare, for instance, his firm translations from Dante's *Inferno* with their unpretentious strength and masculine grace, particularly his rendering of the Paulo and Francesca love scene (Canto V, 70 - 142) in *Stories From the Italian Poets*, with his own *Rimini* drawn from the same source;[137] the differences are striking. And yet Hunt achieves the spirit of the original without suppressing his own genuine poetic talent. He agreed, he said, with Voltaire's argument that in translating " 'the letter . . . killeth; but the spirit giveth life.' "[138]

The best of his numerous translations come from a wide range of Italian authors whom he particularly admired, and from the Greeks, especially Homer. He also translated from Latin and French. Hunt loved and respected the "long organ music of Homer" and was contemptuous of Pope's "elegant mistake" which turns, he claimed, "the Dodonaean oak of his original into such smooth little toys as these—'Rise, son of Peleus! rise *divinely brave*; / *Assist* the combat, and *Patroclus* save!' "[139] Hunt's own translations from the *Iliad* achieve a serious dignity and unpretentious strength rare in his own poetry:

> And when they heard the brazen voice, their minds
> Were all awakened; and the proud-maned horses
> Ran with the chariots round, for they foresaw
> Calamity; and the charioteers were smitten,

When they beheld the ever-active fire
Upon the dreadful head of the great-minded one,
Burning; for bright-eyed Pallas made it burn.
Thrice o'er the trench divine Achilles shouted;
And thrice the Trojans and their great allies
Rolled back; and twelve of all their noblest men
Then perished, crushed by their own arms and chariots.[140]

We can only agree with Thorpe's wish that Hunt had left us a complete Homer that had the quality of his excellent fragments.[141] Moreover, English-speaking readers would be considerably enriched had Hunt rendered the entire *Divine Comedy*.

D. G. Rossetti, himself an excellent translator, proclaimed Hunt "the greatest translator England has produced."[142] This praise is too generous, yet most students of this demanding art warmly admire Hunt's contributions. Despite his linguistic competence, his catholic taste, his respect for the original, and his poetic talent, he failed to become the century's foremost translator chiefly because of the fragmentary and limited nature of his work in this field and perhaps also because of his predilection toward the gentler and lighter moments in great literature. In the long run, his most significant contribution may have been his help in creating popular interest in what we have since come to call "comparative literature," and thus in reducing insular attitudes in art. He was especially active in the dissemination of Italian literature, always an important part of his own life and the development of his taste.[143]

Hunt, good critic that he was, anticipated our judgment of him. As early as 1832 he admitted being sure only of his "admiration of genius in others"; of his own work, he realized that "pretension is nothing; the performance everything."[144] He noted that Sir John Suckling's "Ballad on a Wedding" was "small and unambitious," yet it was an "unmisgiving and happy production" doing what it set out to do so well that it had outlived more heroic offerings. So too with William Shenstone's "School Mistress"; it was humble in every sense "except its humane and thoughtful sweetness."[145] If Hunt had not always practiced what he observed in these authors and achieved their perfection, he at least now knew where his "station" was:

I please myself with thinking, that had the circumstances of my life permitted it, I might have done something a little worthier of acceptance, in the way of a mixed kind of narrative poetry, part lively and part serious, somewhere between the longer poems of the Italians, and the *Fabliaux* of the old French. My propensity would have been (and, oh! had my duties permitted, how willingly would I have passed my life in it! how willingly now pass it!) to write 'eternal new stories' in verse, of no great length, but just sufficient to vent the pleasure with which I am stung on meeting with some touching adventure, and which haunts me till I can speak of it somehow. [146]

We may interpret these life circumstances differently than did Hunt, but this wistful account does describe the poems he could and did occasionally write.

CHAPTER 3

# *Dramatic Critic*

## I  *Reviewer*

IF Hunt is correct in his recollections, a performance of Franklin's *Egyptian Festival* in March 1800 marked his first experience as a playgoer. Yet he was a professional drama critic by 1805, and he had published by 1808 his *Critical Essays on the Performers of the London Theatres.* In the twenty-seven or so years following 1805, he wrote over six hundred theatrical papers and reviews; and, except for two periods, he was almost continuously involved with such criticism. No other contemporary man of letters whose interests and activities were as widespread as Hunt's had more concern for the stage. Despite its contemporary degradation, the genre remained for him prestigious because "the drama is the most perfect imitation of human life; by means of the stage it represents man in all his varieties of mind, his expressions of manner, and his power of action, and is the first of moralities because it teaches us in the most impressive way the knowledge of ourselves."[1]

Hunt did not, as some critics suggest, invent theatrical criticism; for, by the start of the nineteenth century, newspaper coverage was taken for granted. But Hunt claimed that, at the outset of his career, such coverage as existed lacked any depth or integrity whatsoever. Free dinners, free tickets, and prejudicial business relationships so reduced critical objectivity that the reviewer was only "permitted to find out that a bad play was not good, or an actress's petticoat of lawful dimensions."[2] According to Hunt, such a critic's loyalties were not to his readers but to his hosts: "what the public took for criticism on a play was a draft upon the box-office, or reminiscences of last Thursday's salmon and lobster-sauce."[3] Writing of this period in his autobiography so many years later,

Hunt might be expected to have exaggerated, but numerous examples abound of the kind of notices Hunt describes: "The custom was, to write as short and as favourable a paragraph on the new piece as could be; to say that Bannister was 'excellent' and Mrs. Jordan 'charming'; to notice the 'crowded house' or invent it, if necessary; and to conclude by observing that "the whole went off with *eclat*'. For the rest, it was a critical religion in those times to admire Mr. Kemble: and at the period in question Master Betty had appeared, and been hugged to the hearts of the town as the young Roscius."[4] In 1805, no one expected an objective review, but, by 1832, when Hunt had ceased writing theatrical papers, such objectivity was firmly established.

Hunt became theatrical critic for his brother John's *News* when the publication was begun in 1805. Less flamboyant than Leigh, John nonetheless shared his younger brother's vigorous intellectual independence, as their subsequent political jousts with the Prince Regent and their ensuing imprisonment indicated. They recognized a need for such independence in theatrical criticism as well as in political commentary; and, once the principle had been established, they rapidly acquired a reputation for being their own men. This view was Hunt's, and it was shared by many contemporaries who considered Hunt highly influential in the establishment of reputable theatrical criticism.[5] He was followed by two abler and eventually more famous critics in this genre—Lamb and Hazlitt—but he had been a pioneer. Perhaps here, where his contribution was the most original, he has been least recognized. These papers, like so much he wrote, suffered the fate of transient journalism; however, his impact on the quality of the theater was felt more permanently.

## II   *The Degraded Stage*

In literary criticism, Hunt was primarily an introducer and educator; in theatrical criticism, he was also a reformer of, as he acknowledged, "a most unfortunate period of the stage."[6] No major Romantic author invested much energy in a genre long since debased, although several wrote closet dramas. Theatrical fare usually consisted, therefore, of traditionally successful pieces (often badly mutilated), of plays by contemporary hacks, and of extravaganzas. In 1808, Hunt looked with horror upon "the utter deformity of the modern drama,"[7] a view shared by Byron in his *English Bards and*

*Scotch Reviewers.* Hunt crushingly criticized not only actors, managers, and critics but also such modern play "mechanics" as comic writers Andrew Cherry, Frederic Reynolds, Thomas Dibdin, William Lewis, and Samuel Arnold. In an appendix to *Critical Essays*, Hunt analyzed the "appearances, causes, and consequences of the decline of British comedy"; and he explained and lamented the popularity of such writers.[8]

He regarded in this analysis the problem of theatrical offerings and audience taste as a cultural vicious circle. The owners of theaters (like television producers today) argued then that they simply satisfied the demands of their audiences. In 1811, when Hunt reviewed the elder George Colman's melodrama *Blue Beard*, he considered it "one of those wretched compounds of pun and parade, which serve to amuse the great babies of this town."[9] The play did not warrant review, Hunt noted, except for the fact that "horse actors" had invaded "classical" Covent Garden, which thereby indicated the degree to which the theater had to share the blame for the "corrupted taste" of theatergoers. By staging such works, the theater "materially helps to produce that corruption." Eventually "these spectators learn to like nothing else; and then the managers must administer to their depraved appetite, or they cannot get rich."[10] These "spectacles and hyppodramas" were clearly responsible for the "vitiated state of the public taste."[11]

Hunt assumes in this criticism (as he does in his literary criticism) that genuine artistry will bring its audience along with it. The theaters, however, choose expedience: ". . . an elephant can dispense with delicacy of inspection; and storms, murders, Newgate-Calendar plots, shipwrecks, crashes of music, dogs, horses, real water, anything, in short, but real plays, are at length not only tolerated but desired by the public, out of an instinctive sense that they are the best things which the houses are fit for."[12]

In 1806, while still charged with the reformer's zeal, Hunt noted that the situation that Oliver Goldsmith had lamented—the revival of old plays at the expense of modern playwrights—had reversed; he argued that "we are presented with the hasty comedies, or rather with nothing but the bloated farces of mercenary writers" who, as "journeyman mechanic[s]" work in the factory owned by "the depraver of public taste, and consequently of public morals."[13] Moreover, "with respect to a tragic writer, the stage seems to be utterly hopeless" since Miss Joanna Baillie, despite her talents, writes in her *Plays on the Passions* "poetical dialogue rather than tragedies."[14]

Hunt, concerned with drama as performance rather than as literature, urged the essential nature of "plot and action."[15] Some years later in a review of the publication of Robert Dallas' tragedies *Fulvius Valens* and *Adrastus*, Hunt observed that these plays shared two of the typical flaws of modern tragedy in their lack of significant action and of real people whom we can admire but, more important, feel with.[16] These two deficiencies produced static, languid plays, and, in its search for action, the audience was driven to patronize extravaganzas.[17]

In a sea of spectacle, cheap farce, and stillborn tragedy, there existed islands of great drama; and chief among such refuges were the plays of Shakespeare which provided the standard and held out the hope for what the theater could be. Rare as they were, they established Hunt's goal: to see "What you ought to see in an English Theatre—an excellent drama properly performed and properly appreciated."[18] Nor did he ever lose hope. After reviewing for twenty-six years during one of the saddest periods in the history of the English stage, Hunt could still be optimistic. Despite the "supposed decline of a taste for the drama,"[19] he saw reasons to believe that theatrical reviewing would be considerably more pleasant in ten years:

An existing drama springs out of the nature of the times. . . . The mind of the age has been again shaken up by the revival of noble doctrines, by the diffusion of that knowledge of which his Lordship [Lord Brougham, the Lord Chancellor] has been so eminent a promoter, and by the glorious example of the second French revolution, which has exhibited the social virtues in a new and almost unhoped-for light, and given confidence to the noblest expectations. On all these accounts, and in common with every other improvement, the drama is likely to revive.[20]

### III   *Critical Motives, Approaches, and Values*

But early in the century Hunt apparently did not see many signs of hope for the stage. When defending his *Examiner* papers against the accusation that he was overly harsh, Hunt not only succinctly stated his attitude governing theatrical reviewing but generally described his critical approach: "Ill-nature wishes to inflict pain; severity, or what is so called in this instance, is nothing but a wish to speak the truth belonging to its office, to consider many interests instead of one—nay, to consider that one also, and eventually to save pain."[21] It is true that Hunt's attacks were occasionally none too gentle. His tight little essay about a mock melodrama by Dibdin ends with a clever application of the old fable of the jackass who, since he was carrying holy relics, thought the crowd's applause was for him. The essay bluntly exposes lies in the playbill, explains the mock-heroic, demonstrates Dibdin's piece to be neither mock-heroic nor burlesque, and summarizes the work as the "most stupid piece of impertinence that has disgraced the English stage for some years past."[22] To Hunt, the "debauch of merriment" produced by Dibdin might have historical sources; but Hunt thought that the "great *existing* reason" was "the mere want of critical opposition."[23] Hunt has faith in the efficacy of the critical lash he lays on; hence, his vigor.

He was not, of course, always so unrelentingly harsh. But most of his early papers are marked by an intensity that stemmed from his very considerable enthusiasm for all aspects of the theater. One of the most basic and attractive qualities of his work is the vividness with which he portrays his theatrical world. Because of his desire to introduce and share, he gives us wonderful firsthand accounts of such famous artists as Nicolò Paganini, or what it is like to attend a performance at Covent Garden during the Old Price riots when the crowd demonstrated wildly against ticket increases.[24] Because of his focus on dramatic performance, a sense of place is of paramount importance to his review. The redecoration of Drury Lane, for instance, brings him joy with its new gas lights which characteristically put him "in mind of what one fancies in poetry, of the flamy breath at the point of a Seraph's wand." In order to give his audience a sharp sense of the actual experience of playgoing, he often reconstructs the visual aspect of whole scenes, especially comic ones.

Concreteness, then, is perhaps his chief characteristic. Recent editors of his dramatic criticism point out that "in a day when much dramatic criticism was mere foggy generalization, Hunt was specific." In addition to the reading public, "actors, authors, and stage managers alike found in his criticism something tangibly useful."[25] Hunt objected to Dr. Johnson's criticism because, though it contained very reasonable generalizations, it remained "careless of all proof."[26] His own writings are the reverse of this. Unlike Johnson, Hunt neither lived in an age of critical absolutes nor was able to create his own. Confident of his taste, articulate and specific in his examples, he was nonetheless subjective. His success as a reviewer resulted not from the application of esthetic principles (though he was not completely devoid of them) but from the qualities Landré so aptly catalogues—"lucidity and detach-ment—the independence, the fairness, the sense of justice that were to make him famous as political writer for the *Examiner*"[27]—and, finally, from his own inherent good taste.

Hunt's approach to dramatic analysis and evaluation is founded on theory even less than is his literary criticism, but we find some implicit references to neo-Classical standards in his early work. For example, in discussing the lamentable state of modern tragedy in *Classic Tales*, Hunt cites the Aristotelian proposition that action, not character, is at the heart of a performance, and he notes the static quality of Joanna Baillie's tragedies.[28] Unlike Byron, however, Hunt makes almost no appeal to such guidelines as the neo-Classical unities of action, time, and place. Moreover, he frequently vents his disgust for the "French School" (the Augustans) which meant, "dramatically speaking—pompous, frigid, and ranting."[29] His contempt was that of the Romantic who was convinced of the "French School's" hostility toward Shakespeare. Consequently, Johnson, who personified that school to Hunt, is constantly at-tacked. When Johnson is unable to explain his appreciation of Falstaff, Hunt argues, he covers his failure with declamation.[30] Similarly, Hunt feels that Doctor Johnson's opinion of *Timon of Athens* "is a mere dove-tailing of words, or to speak after his own fashion, a smooth adjustment of alliterative antithesis."[31] When Johnson (applying an essentially Romantic criterion) derogates *Julius Caesar* on the grounds that he has "never been strongly agitated in perusing it" and therefore finds it "somewhat cold and unaffecting," Hunt replies that such an unsupported generalization not only betrays Johnson's critical methods but also illustrates his "absolute unfitness for poetical criticism, at least with regard to works of a higher order."[32]

By contrast, Hunt recognizes and has the warmest regard for the dramatic criticism of Lamb, Hazlitt, and A. W. Schlegal. Hunt naturally associated himself with these writers, since he largely shared their Romantic bias. (By 1831, Hunt would declare Lamb and Hazlitt to be by far the two best dramatic critics that England had produced.[33]) Yet Hunt shows a curious blindness to Coleridge, who had become the leader of Romantic criticism, and though Hunt attended at least one of Coleridge's famous lectures on Shakespeare, he showed no signs of being impressed. In the *Ex-aminer*, February 9, 1812, Hunt criticized Coleridge as a critic, possibly with these lectures in mind.

## IV  *Shakespeare*

Not surprisingly, the context of Hunt's reference to these Romantic critics is almost always Shakespeare. Rightmindedness on the subject of England's greatest writer was for Hunt and other Romantics the surest mark of a critic's intellectual, esthetic, and spiritual strength. Because of these mutual concerns, Hunt declared Hazlitt "the first to do justice to Shakespeare's characters in general."[34] Hazlitt's *Characters of Shakespeare's Plays*, which evoked this approval, had also been reviewed by Francis Jeffrey, who snidely suggested that Hazlitt's motive had been to "show extraordinary love" rather than "extraordinary knowledge."[35] Hunt asserts that "love, in this instance, is knowledge"; and he appreciates the rarity of "having Shakespeare so well understood as well as admired. . . ."[36] It is much to Hunt's credit that he was one of the first as a writer to promote Hazlitt and as editor to employ him; and, though their friendship suffered a considerable reduction in warmth as years passed, Hunt retained the deepest respect for Hazlitt and his works, such as *Lectures on the Literature of the Age of Elizabeth*.[37]

Several months following his review of Hazlitt's book, Hunt declared the German critic A. W. Schlegel to be, "with the exception of a few scattered criticisms from Mr. Lamb . . . the only writer who seemed truly to *understand* as well as feel" Shakespeare.[38] Hunt, who apparently read no German, probably learned to know Schlegel's influential *Lectures on Dramatic Art and Literature* through John Black's 1815 English translation.

Hunt's approval of critics such as these, along with his opposition to Johnson and the "French School," clearly indicates that his theoretical bias, insofar as he had one, was essentially Romantic. Some critics have even argued that Hunt "gave impetus to the English Romantic Movement by his adoption of romantic criteria in certain reviews for the *Examiner*."[39] But Hunt's role as Romantic theorist and popularizer emerged later in his career, whereas his most influential dramatic criticism came early. However, if he had not consciously adopted and decided to disseminate the new theory, his sympathies with it were instinctive, as his attitude toward Shakespeare illustrates.

The Romantic period was not the first to worship Shakespeare; the last third of the eighteenth century saw the marked growth of that devotion.[40] A chief characteristic of the Romantic attitude, however, was to make total commitment to Shakespeare an index of a critic's esthetic and even spiritual trustworthiness. Fleece argues that Hunt, despite his Romantic excesses, "never falls completely under the spell of the Romantic enthusiasm for Shakespeare." He points out that Hunt was generally opposed to the "Romantic Heresy" of thinking Shakespeare better read than seen, and he contends that⁵ Hunt's position suggests a "transition from the eighteenth century's rationally hesitant admiration and the bardolatry of Hunt's contemporaries."⁴¹ It is probably true that Hunt's early attitude was in part an unthinking application of older, more conservative values. But by 1820 Hunt treats Shakespeare not simply as the best of English poets but virtually as a divine being.

In a piece written on the occasion of Shakespeare's birthday, Hunt sounds more like a priest than a man of letters; the essay is a kind of religious celebration of the bard's ascension. Shakespeare is "alive" now spiritually, and a bust of him in a hypothetical ceremony "would look like the 'present deity' of the occasion." To such an event everyone would bring some favorite quotation, piously "laying it before his image."⁴² Hunt was not entirely fanciful in this adulation. One does not criticize a god; he assumes the error is in himself. Hence a play like *King John*, says Hunt, again attacking Johnson, is as good as the subject demanded it to be since it contains "all that is adequate to a just and delicate discrimination of character," as well as Shakespeare's "equable" and "elegant" "flow of versification."⁴³

The failure of such critics as Johnson, Hunt argued, lay in their limited vision of Shakespeare's created world—one that was for Hunt, as Stout points out, "the all-inclusive Nature of the Romantic poets."⁴⁴ Johnson did not recognize the "universal and still sager world of the poet" because his own was limited "exclusively" to "the Strand, hypochondria, charity, bigotry, wit, argument, and a good dinner; a pretty region, but not the green as *well* as smoky world of Nature and Shakespeare."⁴⁵ Hunt, for example, saw *Julius Caesar* as "of itself a whole school of human nature."⁴⁶ He was nervous about Shakespeare's apparent failure to applaud any of his own contemporaries, and he had trouble appreciating the history plays because of his own political liberalism.⁴⁷ But Hunt's typical role is that of worshipper: "The more this immortal poet is considered the more he will be found superior to all times and circumstances"; he is a poet who, making us transcend our narrow prejudices, elevates us to "involuntary philosophers" capable of realizing our true humanity.⁴⁸

Hunt's almost religious sanctification of "our great bard," as much as his scholarship, makes him repudiate any editorial adulteration of Shakespeare's original plays. In 1808, we find him angrily reviewing the Covent Garden revival of *King Lear* "as it was altered by Tate, who was altered by Coleman, who was altered by Garrick."[49] Hunt's specific objection (beyond his outrage at profaning the sacred) is the justifiable complaint against having the play's tragic impact destroyed: "Shakespeare made his play end unhappily, because he knew that real nature required such a catastrophe." Amusing, however, is Hunt's blindness in the midst of good sense when he could forgive Tate for a few little changes such as "to omit the *Fool* which is now out of date" and possibly the offstage blinding of Gloucester as well.[50] Nor, right or wrong, did he object to the introduction of music in Covent Garden's 1820 revival of the *Twelfth Night.*[51]

But these are exceptions; typically, we find him rejecting such alterations as a change in the death scene of *Romeo and Juliet*[52] or in Drury Lane's production of *Richard, Duke of York*, actually a version of *King Henry VI*. His reasonable objection in the latter example was to the adaptor's violation of the original play's integrity, a violation that produced only "a strange and feeble compound out of scenes and characters." "Disjointing a great poet in this manner" can end only by "turning beauty to deformity, and strength to weakness."[53] What success is achieved, the adaptor in his vanity assumes to be his; but it is actually the work's remaining vitality that is felt—even in its ruin.[54]

## V  *Dramatic Taste*

With drama as with other art forms, Hunt's taste was catholic. He shared his age's reverence for the Classical theater, and he not only admired Shakespeare but in numerous small ways helped to promote contemporary interest in other Elizabethan and Jacobean dramatists as well. As a reviewer, he was limited by the infrequent performance of non-Shakespearean Renaissance drama; as a reader, by the scarcity of texts. However, he took every occasion to share his enthusiasm for what he considered one of the world's two great bodies of drama, just as in his role as literary critic he constantly reintroduced his readers to Renaissance literature in general. As early as 1805, he was writing about Francis Beaumont and John Fletcher;[55] later, he reviewed productions of Christopher Marlowe and Philip Massinger.[56] In *Imagination and Fancy* (1844) and *Wit and Humour* (1846), he discusses Ben Jonson, Thomas Middleton, Thomas Decker, John Webster, and John Ford. Prefatory to his *The Descent of Liberty* (1815), he writes a long "Account of the Origin and Nature of Masks," recognizing that, "as the species of dramatic production called a Mask has been unknown among us for a long time, the reader may not be unwilling . . . to hear a few words respecting it."[57] Hunt concludes a review of Marlowe's *Jew of Malta* with the recommendation that readers unacquainted with Marlowe and his peers refer to the "Collections of the Ancient British Drama, to some separate old plays lately published, and to that excellent work, Lamb's *Specimens of English Dramatic Poets*" as well as to the recently collected writing of Lamb himself.[58]

Hunt's attitude toward Restoration drama changed radically during his lifetime. Early in his career, he rejected these plays on moral grounds and saw modern productions of them, even when expurgated, as "scattering a pestilence from the graves of departed geniuses."[59] By 1840, however, he had edited *The Dramatic Works of Wycherley, Congreve, Vanbrugh, and Farquhar;* and, when Victorian Thomas Macaulay reviewed the edition, he chastized Hunt for rejecting the charge of immorality normally brought against the Restoration theater.[60] Hunt, whose taste for comic drama exceeded his appreciation of the tragic, had learned to appreciate the wit and humor of a sophisticated age.

About eighteenth century drama, Hunt was naturally more severe; he admired a few authors but ignored the bulk. He considered Sheridan's *The Rivals* and *School for Scandal*, Oliver Goldsmith's *She Stoops to Conquer*, and a few of O'Keefe's plays the best of the period.[61] Despite his regard for *She Stoops to Conquer*, Hunt argued that the decline of English comedy into farce began when Goldsmith, in "indignant haste," overthrew sentimental comedy: "The farce succeeded, the extravagant though delightful vagaries of *She Stoops to Conquer*, like the touch of the painter, turned the weeping face of the town into a laughing one; O'Keefe, a man of much humour, afterwards kept up the peal, till it became mere noise and grimace with Mr. Reynolds and his brother merry-andrews Messrs. Dibdin and Cherry."[62] And though Hunt termed sentimental comedy "solemn foppery," he objected to Goldsmith's extreme reaction.[63] Moreover, in 1810 Hunt speaks respectfully of Richard Steele's *Conscious Lovers* as "the best sentimental comedy in the language." In the same review, he hopes the vulgarity of contemporary taste can be ameliorated so that "the town . . . can relish the delicate character and graceful sentiment of our purer dramatists."[64] He admires Steele's piece not for its wit, which he acknowledges is not prominent, but for its delicacy and reasonableness, and for "the insights into human nature of that nice and feeling discrimination which is the first characteristic of Steele's writings."[65]

Although we have already indicated Hunt's reaction to the drama of his own day and his hope for the future, few writers of any talent were devoting their powers to the stage. Therefore, when Thomas Moore chose to write an opera (*M.P.; or The Blue Stocking*, 1811), Hunt was prepared to applaud it; for, "seated . . . immeasurably above the dramatists of the day, and qualified to enlighten the sphere below him with his brilliant powers," Moore was sure to help improve popular taste and help overcome the "degraded condition of the modern drama."[66] But, when Hunt attended the performance, he discovered that Moore had not raised esthetic standards; rather, he had "condescended to mingle with those imitative cattle," and had produced "an unambitious, undignified, and most unworthy compilation of pun, equivoque, and clap-trap!"[67] Though the work was somewhat above the usual English farce, it supplied bad contemporary dramatists "with a most afflicting excuse for their awkward frisks and vagaries."[68]

Nor, with one understandable exception, did Hunt appreciate the stillborn closet dramas of his great contemporaries who, choosing to remain aloof from the unpleasant realities of the working theater, yet wished to write in the form. The exception was the *Cenci*, written by Shelley and dedicated to Hunt himself. Shelley's play is now generally admitted to be the best of all Romantic attempts at drama. Unlike Byron, who argued against the use of Renaissance models, Hunt finds his pleasure in the play increased by such associations. About Shelley's dramatic talent he had no doubt: "had he lived, he would have been the greatest dramatic writer since the days of Elizabeth, if indeed he has not abundantly proved himself such in his tragedy of the *Cenci*."[69]

## VI  *The Art of Acting*

Not just poetic immortality recommended Shakespeare and other great dramatists to Hunt; his approval is generally based on a play's actability, and this quality is achieved by "giving proper characters their proper language." On the other hand, wretched modern dramas, especially the comedies, were characterized by their "want of natural connection between the speakers and the dialogue."[70] His worship of Shakespeare led him to argue occasionally that no actor could finally do justice to his characters since even "the finest musical instrument is insufficient to supply all the effect of a great writer for a band,"[71] but this view was an exaggeration of his usual position. The statement indicates, however, the central role of acting in his theatrical reviews.

Much of the originality and pioneering quality of Hunt's reviews results, in fact, from the seriousness with which he approached acting. Although he recognized acting to be (like his own journalism) a perishable art, he recognized its splendid potential and thought it worthy of nurture. Consequently, he is much more acting-oriented than the greater Romantic critics of the theater. In the preface to his significantly titled *Critical Essays on the Performers of the London Stage*, Hunt relates how, in the wasteland of contemporary drama, he had discovered that his main pleasure had often "arisen from the actors totally abstracted from the author."[72] Dramatists, recognizing their own inferiority, often wrote plays for the actors; and they reversed, therefore, the appropriate relationship. The miracle to Hunt was that the actors could make performances as enjoyable as they did, but he attributed their success to "this strange superiority of the mimetic over the literary part of the stage, of the organ in fact over its inspirer, that determined me to criticize the actors."[73]

His criticism was as independent about actors as about the whole subject of the theater. Popular reputations did not sway him; his general notion of what was wanted of an actor seems to have been clearer than his principles governing the larger issues of dramatic merit. The late nineteenth century drama critic William Archer saw three general steps in Hunt's criticism of an actor's performance: first, to establish the character's nature as the dramatist intended it; second, to test the actor's performance against the conception and against the performances of other talented actors; and third, to discuss the performance in concrete particularity.[74] This final stage of Hunt's review accounts for the vivid sense of place and for the living presence that often make his reviews interesting reading even now. This aspect of his criticism also accounts for the pragmatic value his opinions had for at least some contemporary actors. The youthful critic was referred to as "the damned boy" by one disgruntled popular actor; but Charles Mathews, whose role as Sir Fretful Plagiary had been praised by Hunt, later spoke of him as "the greatest dramatic critic of that day . . . whose judgment was universally sought and received as infallible by all actors and lovers of the drama."[75] Despite Mathews' undoubtedly biased opinion, other contemporary reactions about Hunt's freshness, vigorous candor, and genuine insight indicate that he was a force to be contended with. Apparently at least one dramatist must have recognized his authority, as the following note in 1808 suggests: "A Farce in two Acts, entitled *Antiquity*, is in the Press, written upon the dramatic principles inculcated by the author of the theatrical criticism in the *News*, to whom it is dedicated."[76]

The test of the actual against the ideal performance was justified, Hunt felt, by what he saw as the great unused potential in actors. The actor is an artist; as in the poet, the actor's employment of imagination, not simply reason (and hence imitation), accounts for an inspired performance. He applied this typically Romantic assumption especially to the performance of weak modern drama which, unlike Shakespearean drama, for instance, threw the burden of success largely on the actors: "*Imagination* is an original and active power, that forms its own images and impresses them upon the minds of others: it belongs therefore more to the *poet*. But actors have sometimes to imagine as well as to conceive, for if the suggestions of the poet are few and feeble, they must be invigorated by the additional ideas of the actor, who in this instance *imagines* as well as *conceives*."[77]

This faculty was especially valuable to tragic actors since, though it is easier to attain mediocrity in that genre, it is much more difficult to achieve greatness. Successful comedy depends upon being able to reproduce more of the character's habits than his passions; but, since tragic actors must reproduce passions, "the idea of passion . . . requires more imagination than that of habit." Hence for the tragic performer "imagination . . . is the great test of genius."[78] The successful tragic actor "possesses a more *poetical* genius than the comedian," and Hunt reminds us that the poetical "always indicates the highest genius."[79] Nevertheless, a comic actor "requires no common fancy," Hunt argues, (in an apparent imagination-fancy distinction that prefigures his later Romantic theory); for this actor's primary faculty must be "an instantaneous perception of everything that varies from the general seriousness of human nature. . . ."[80] Hunt's priorities are clear: "in the polite arts imagination is always more esteemed than humour: humour presents us with visible objects;" but imagination, on the other hand, " 'bodies forth forms of things unseen. . . .' "[81]

But these requirements were claimed in 1808 at the height of Hunt's interest in acting; generally, his criterion for a good performance was less elevated since he objected chiefly to the "artificial style of the actors lately in vogue." He was upset to discover in Edmund Kean's performance of Richard III only the success of the "ordinary, stagy class" of actors:

> We expected to find in Mr. Kean an actor as little artificial as possible; we expected to find no declamation, no common rant, no puttings forth of the old oratorical right hand, no speech-making and attitudinizing at one, no implication, in short, of a set of spectators; but something genuine and unconscious, something that moved, looked, and spoke solely under the impulse of the immediate idea. . . .

> If this should be thought too much to demand in tragedy, it is only because we have been accustomed to the reverse—to art instead of nature.[82]

Hunt is actually saying that, in this instance, Kean is no better than John Phillip Kemble, "the best kind of actor in the artificial style."[83] Four years later (1819) when Hunt is comparing William Charles Macready with Kean, we find that his expectations are the reverse of the above instance. Led to anticipate "vagueness and generality" as well as "declamation" from Macready, Hunt is delighted to find the "truth of detail" and "thoughts giving a soul to words."[84] Kean is seen in this instance as having first given "the living stage that example of a natural style of acting, on which Mr. Macready has founded his new rank in the theatrical world."[85]

Again and again in Hunt's reviews, declamation, eloquence, and rant (or coquetry in actresses) are scorned; a "natural tone" is necessary since "people do not admire a passage merely because it is unlike others, but because it is like Nature"[86] and since no other way exists to hold an audience with integrity. Initially at least, Hunt made a distinction here between comic and tragic actors. In *Critical Essays*, he argues that the "loftier persons of tragedy require an elevation of language and manner, which they never use in real life."[87] Naturalness for the tragic actor, therefore, consists in fidelity to "the general opinion of life and manners," not to any "too natural simplicity of manner" any more than to declamation.[88] As time went on, however, Hunt's reviews tended to mute this distinction.

For the Keans, Kembles, and Macreadys, Hunt advised a form of "method acting" in which it was essential for the actor to project into the life of the character—to study that character so carefully that to be him was to be himself. To Hunt, the difference between Kemble and Mrs. Siddons is that, where the former often "studiously meditates a step or an attitude in the midst of passion," Mrs. Siddons never needs to think about such particular manifestations of character "and therefore is always natural, because on occasions of great feeling it is the passions should influence the actions. . . ."[89] At times, Hunt allowed this theory to place an unreasonable burden on the actor. Since *King Lear* portrayed for Hunt the definitive tragic experience, the definitive test of the tragic actor's abilities was exacting: "An actor who performs *Lear* truly, should so terrify and shake the town, as to be requested never to perform the part again. If he does this, he does it well. If not, he does not do it at all. There is no medium, in a scene which we are to witness with our *eyes*, between an unbearable *Lear*, and no *Lear*."[90] Here again Hunt nearly falls into the Romantic fallacy about Shakespeare's unactability mentioned earlier. But elsewhere, especially when reviewing non-Shakespearean roles, he is more reasonable. His comments on drama retain their interest, not just for the actor or theatrical historian, but also for the student of English literature. In these discussions he is often at his best—witty, pungent, imaginative, and nearly always vital. And in these essays an ill-formed or missing theory is easily overcome by his talent for specificity.

## VII   *Opera and Music*

In addition to legitimate drama, Hunt naturally reviewed various musical performances but with less regularity. He damned with faint praise a production of John Gay's *The Beggar's Opera* apparently because he associated it with the "vulgarity" of the "French School" he so disliked, the same influence that had "kept down and depraved" the imagination of Pope.[91] But Hunt was normally not so harsh on musical performances. When the first English production of Rossini's *The Barber of Seville* failed to live up to its continental reputation, Hunt complained only mildly and hoped the composer young enough to grow into distinction.[92] Of Mozart, he had the highest regard; and he was one of the very first English critics to write extensively about him.[93] He warmly praises *Don Giovanni* (and devotes much of his review to a discussion of sound and its relationship to the supernatural); but, in reviews of *Figaro*, he gives himself up to such unparaphraseable judgments as "all is a smoothing interchange of enjoyments—a series of sprightly turns of lapping pleasures,"[94] or a descriptive summary of the action. He is more interesting when he is evoking the great violinist Paganini (about whom he also wrote some pleasing blank verse), "that wonderful person" who brought to life any stage on which he performed.[95]

Oddly enough, given his temperament, Hunt appears somewhat less enthusiastic about the ballet; and he is even less moved by oratorios. Reviewing Handel's *Messiah* in 1831, he complained of the "sombre and unvaried" effect which produced an inappropriate pain. "Music is a pleasurable art," he argued, "even in its melancholy, and should not deal with many continuous thoughts more painful than amount to pensiveness."[96] Elsewhere he referred to the oratorio's "pretence to something devotional without the reality."[97] Beyond his natural good taste, Hunt's qualifications for musical criticism are questionable; but, when he took on the responsibility, such lack of preparation was not unusual.[98]

Hunt's most vigorous and interesting theatrical reviews appeared in the earliest third of his journalistic career. As first political and then literary interests multiplied, Hunt's output and enthusiasm diminished. When the time came for him to try his own hand at playwriting, he no doubt recalled the days when as "the damned boy" he had scourged the theater from across the safety of the footlights. In later years when he preferred introducing his readers to art rather than subjecting art to critical harshness, he admitted the shortcomings of reviewing: "Never, after I had taken critical pen in hand, did I pass the thoroughly delightful evenings at the playhouse which I had done when I went only to laugh or be moved. I had the pleasure, it is true, of praising those whom I admired; but the retributive uneasiness of the very pleasure of blaming attended it."[99] But, whatever Hunt's personal unpleasantness, he had helped dramatic criticism develop from its primitive origins in theatrical notices to a refined and useful art.

CHAPTER 4

# Prose Man and Editor

I F a major poetic success was to elude Leigh Hunt, a firm place in the world of contemporary letters was still to be his. Despite his early and continued publication of poetry, he first made his impact as a drama critic and as an essayist—originally for his brother John's *News* in 1805 and then in their jointly produced *Examiner* starting in 1808. Destined to remain a minor poet, Hunt was to become as a professional prose man one of his generation's best-known literary figures.

## I *Journalist*

The weekly *Examiner* opens and the quarterly *Liberal* (1822-1823) closes the most impressive period in Hunt's career as essayist and editor, a period of fifteen uninterrupted years of prose effort. The *Examiner,* perhaps the best and certainly the most famous of Hunt's journals, ran from 1808 - 1821 under Hunt (and continued for many years without him). Published in 1810 and 1811, Hunt's *Reflector* has been described as one of the first distinctly literary periodicals—"the cradle of the familiar essay in the nineteenth century"[1]—and it may be said to have given Lamb his start as an essayist. While editing the curious annual *Literary Pocket Book* (1819 - 1823), Hunt was also turning out his weekly *Indicator* (1819 - 1821), a periodical designed "to notice any subjects whatsoever within the range of the editor's knowledge or reading," his business being largely "with honey in the old woods."[2] The *Liberal,* which Hunt produced with Byron in Italy after the death of the third partner, Shelley, ran for four numbers in 1822 - 1823. This periodical, which advocated "every species of liberal knowledge" and attacked "the instincts of selfish choice,"[3] published among other well-known works Byron's brilliant "Vision of Judgment," Hazlitt's "My First Acquaintance with Poets," Shelley's "Song, Written for an Indian Air," and many contributions by Hunt himself. Brief and uneven as it was, the *Liberal* was nonetheless one of the highest quality periodicals in the early nineteenth century.

In the next twenty-three years (1828 - 1851), Hunt edited and wrote for six more journals. The weekly *Companion* of 1828 contains excellent essays of the *Indicator* variety and takes up again the "Books, Politics, and Theatricals" of the earlier journals. The political writing in *Companion* is gentler than that of the *Examiner* of twenty years earlier; for anyone "desirous of becoming acquainted with anything that concerns mankind at large" politics may be seen to be "a part of humane literature."[4] The *Chat of the Week* in 1830 with its revealing title was also intended to be eclectic: "we have no limits as to subjects."[5] *Chat* was followed by the fantastic effort of the *Tatler*, a daily that ran for 493 numbers in 1830 - 1832. Although the *Tatler* contained only four folio pages, Hunt, except during periods of illness, was its sole contributor. "Slight as it looked" with its characteristic bits of news, theatrical reviews, and essays political and nonpolitical, Hunt claimed in his *Autobiography* that it "nearly killed me."[6] *Leigh Hunt's London Journal* (1834 - 1835), the *Monthly Repository* (1837 - 1838), and the weekly *Leigh Hunt's Journal* (1850 - 1851) conclude his career as combined essayist-editor. The best of these; the *London Journal*, continued and most clearly enunciated Hunt's concept of journalism's educational role that was found earlier in the *Indicator*, *Companion*, and *Tatler*.

In addition to writing much of the copy for these periodicals, writing his own books, editing others, and composing poetry, Hunt wrote articles over the years for at least twenty-five papers and magazines; and the last of his "occasional" papers appeared in the *Spectator* just eight days before his death in 1859. He had been a prose man for over forty years, and the weight and influence of his journals were distributed over the entire first half of the nineteenth century. The journalistic values that governed them, the moral idealism they illustrated, the fine writing that usually characterized them—all these qualities justify George Saintsbury's claim that "to no single man is the praise of having transformed the eighteenth century magazine, or collection of light miscellaneous essays, into its subsequent form due so much as to Hunt."[7]

## II The Examiner: "*Literary Morals*"

By 1831, Hunt viewed the state of the English press with some satisfaction. He could see defects of course, some "very deplorable ones," but he thought that, on the whole, it was carrying out its duty of leadership.[8] At the outset of his career, however, he could find little indication that the press was meeting its responsibilities. In the *Examiner* of March 6, 1808, Hunt published his "Rules for Newspaper Editors," a bitingly ironic summary of the partisan, materialistic, and dishonest practices of the press that were designed to achieve editorial success.[9] In the following year, his "Newspaper Principles," appearing in the same periodical, took a cool, hard look at the commercial and political biases that he felt controlled the press and produced "kept journalists." Bluntly indicting a hired press, Hunt blamed political dishonesty largely on greed: "the Proprietor of a daily paper would as soon think of getting money by sheer independence as he would of writing an article for the love of good letters or of literary morals."[10]

That Hunt himself had "literary morals" is clear, if by that interesting term he implied the honest and independent use of the press's immense influence. Journalism may be "fugitive writing," but he knew at first hand and feared the harm of which an immoral press was capable. He did not disdain personal success, but both he and John saw the absolute necessity for honest journalism in the task of reforming England's social and political life. For this cause the *Examiner* was established, and it was a weekly paper destined to produce such an impact on contemporary thought as to warrant R. Brimley Johnson's assertion that Hunt was responsible for "the second important era of progress" toward "the modernizing and democratization of journal-newspapers," the first step having been taken by Daniel Defoe.[11] As Hunt relates in his *Autobiography*, he and his brother took the name for their sixteen page weekly from Swift's Tory journal, not for its politics but for its "wit and fine writing." As for the motto of their *Examiner*—"party is the madness of many for the gain of a few"—Hunt at first ascribed it to Swift; but he changed quickly to Pope when he discovered his mistake. The error illustrates his youthful brashness, his relative ignorance, and his willingness to employ a conservative precedent. The choice suggests also his view of himself as a scather of vice, for he had in mind Swift the satirist more than Swift the political essayist. Moreover, the motto also indicates the essentially political nature of the *Examiner*'s origins, a character later to be modified somewhat by Hunt's imprisonment and his "discovery" of Keats and Shelley. To "Politics, Domestic Economy and Theatricals," he eventually added literary criticism; but, even at the beginning of the *Ex-*

*aminer*, its essentially literary and moderate tone distinguished it from other journals.

The main credo of the new journal was independence. As we have already observed, Hunt earned a name for impartiality as a theatrical critic; and he appealed to that reputation in the prospectus to the *Examiner*: "as the Public have allowed the possibility of IMPARTIALITY in that department, we do not see why the same possibility may not be obtained in POLITICS."[12] To help achieve this objective as well as to concentrate the paper's energy and space, Hunt rejected both advertising and, initially, market reports: "the *Examiner* will have as little to do with bulls and raw hides as with lottery-men and wig-makers."[13] And, though the publication's political principles were roughly liberal Whig, the journal sailed its own course. The establishment press naturally accused it of partisanship, but Hunt could claim years later, with as much justification as these cases ever allow, that the *Examiner* had "lived quite alone."[14]

### III   The Examiner:   *Political Philosophy*

However, the *Examiner* lived alone at the center of the political storm. As Hunt argued later, the paper may have had "absolutely no [political] views whatsoever but those of a decent competence and of the public goods";[15] but, since the journal immediately and vigorously associated itself with the liberal reform movement, it received no quarter and appeared to expect none. Twenty-four years before a parliamentary reform bill was to be passed, Hunt campaigned fiercely for that goal; and, among other, often unpopular, causes, he supported an end to Catholic suppression, the reform of criminal law, and the abolition of the slave trade. He criticized the war with France.

Most dangerously, as we have already noted, Hunt pilloried the Prince of Wales, whose personal deportment and whose repudiation of Whig friends upon becoming Prince Regent caused Hunt to anatomize him week after week. The government's four prosecutions and its eventual jailing of the two Hunt brothers for libeling the regent were undoubtedly popular with a great many ordinary Englishmen. But both Coleridge and Wordsworth disliked, in Wordsworth's term, "such injurious writings"; and Southey hoped for a government victory over these dissident journals that would be produced if necessary by a "vigor beyond the law which the exigence requires."[16]

Years were to pass before some readers softened their animosity toward Hunt, and some never forgave "Examiner Hunt." But, if Hunt's name was odious to many, numerous other readers throughout Great Britain respected the *Examiner* for its refreshingly outspoken independence. In 1821, Hunt was still a celebrity to the people of Plymouth, who feted him while he waited there to sail to Italy. "In its early years," as H. C. Baker says, "it was an exhilarating paper to readers who were young, politically disaffected and inclined to things artistic"—men like Charles Cowden Clarke, Keats, and Shelley.[17] In 1812, Bentham estimated the *Examiner*'s circulation at seven to eight thousand copies weekly;[18] many of these issues appear to have been passed around, thus enlarging Hunt's audience still further.

The first three legal proceedings brought against Leigh and John Hunt as editor and publisher of the *Examiner* were for Leigh's discussion of Major Hogan's accusations of graft related to promotion in the Duke of York's regiment (1808); for what was interpreted to be the *Examiner*'s slur against George the Third (1809); and for reprinting several sections of John Scott's attack on military flogging (1810). The fourth set of charges resulted from Hunt's pungent "fat Adonis of fifty" essay on the regent, a paper occasioned by the *Morning Post*'s publication of a poem fulsome with slavish praise for the regent's rather minimal virtues. A small sample of this provocation suffices:

> To Honour, Virtue, Truth, allied—
> The Nation's safeguard and its pride;
> With monarchs of immortal fame
> Shall bright Renown enrol thy name.
> Adonis! in thy shape and face
> A lib'ral heart and Princely grace
> In thee are seen combined. . . .[19]

The following and perhaps most aggressive section of Hunt's response deserves reprinting since it not only also illustrates the nature of Hunt's attacks on the regent but also provides a sample of some of his more vigorous prose:

What person, unacquainted with the true state of the case, would imagine, in reading these astounding eulogies, that this "Glory of the people" was the subject of millions of shrugs and reproaches!—that this "Protector of the arts" had named a wretched foreigner his historical painter, in disparagement or in ignorance of the merits of his own countrymen!—that this "Mecaenas of the age" patronized not a single deserving writer!—that this "Breather of eloquence" could not say a few decent extempore words, if we are to judge, at least, from what he said to his regiment on its embarkation for Portugal!—that this "Conqueror of hearts" was the disappointer of hopes!—that this "Exciter of desire"—this "Adonis in loveliness", was a corpulent man of fifty!—in short, this *delightful, blissful, wise, pleasurable, honourable, virtuous, true,* and *immortal* prince, was a violater of his word, a libertine over head and ears in disgrace, a despiser of domestic ties, the companion of gamblers and demireps, a man who has just closed half a century without one single claim on the gratitude of his country, or the respect of posterity![20]

The Hunts had escaped the first three prosecutions by luck and good legal aid; but, in this essay, they had gone too far. Prior to the audacity of this late February paper, Hunt had continually baited the regent's ministers. Was he, he ironically asked, now so incorrect in his views as to no longer be an enemy to the government? His attacks grew so unrestrained that he even implied hereditary insanity in the royal family, perhaps the only occasion on which Hunt was totally unfair to the regent. Even after the infamous Adonis essay, he refused to leave the regent in peace. Consequently, the legal skill of Brougham, which had served him so well on the previous charge, could not now save the brothers; in fact, that able counselor was himself attacked by the prosecution as part of a depraved ring bent on the destruction of a noble and innocent prince. The revenge that the prince sought was, as we know, exacted; Leigh and John were sentenced to two years imprisonment, fined five hundred pounds, and placed under heavy securities against five years of good behavior following their release. Rejecting mitigation through guarantees of self-restraint, turning down the offer of political pressure, and refusing assistance in paying their fines, the two young reformer-journalists went to separate prisons.

As Woodring has noted, Hunt's continuing pressure after the failure of the government's third action against him illustrates not only his courage but an excess of youthful pride.[21] On what basis, it might be asked, did he consider himself qualified to undertake the political editorials for the *Examiner* in the first place? Despite his enthusiastic involvement in these years, he was not then, nor was he ever to become, a genuinely political animal.[22] He knew little of political science or law; he admitted to having studied closely only Jean Louis de Lolme's *The Constitution of England* and some of

Blackstone's commentaries; but he was soon to read widely in political literature.[23] Nor was there anything in his cheerful, gentle personality that fed on political warfare; he preferred an imaginary Spenserian bower to Whitehall. At twenty-four, he was almost totally without experience in the harsh and dangerous world he was about to enter.

Youthful pride, therefore, does not sufficiently explain his motivation. Despite inconsistencies and some posturing, the reasons for Hunt's willingness to write in this area are more nearly moral than psychological. Beyond merely desiring to be a writer, he wrote because he was an English patriot and, more importantly, because he was a member of the human community. The quality of communal life was the business of every enlightened man; it was too important to be left to the professionals. In that sense, Hunt saw no distinction between writing about literature and writing about politics; they were both part of the larger concern of a man of letters. In this belief, his youthful naiveté naturally cooperated; it is easier to assume experience is unnecessary, or even a hindrance, when one has none. Yet it was finally not the arrogance of immaturity that drove him to risk the prevailing legal severity but two convictions that he never lost, even after his period of political activism was largely over. First, Hunt believed that man should and does progress toward a higher spiritual and hence better social life; and, second, knowing this to be true, he argued that man's duty is to work toward that objective with whatever talents he might possess. If such progress was inhibited by entrenched institutions, then reform was necessary. Morally, a citizen could not simply be a spectator; he had to "shake off all . . . indolence" and act.[24]

In the prospectus to the *Examiner*, Hunt warned about the dangers of the political party: "a wise man knows no party abstracted from its utility."[25] To Hunt, a party man often becomes one either through the careful construction of a political philosophy or more commonly through unthinking adherence to the loyalties of his class or his family. Hunt was too undisciplined for the first course and seemingly too independent for the second. Yet, despite Hunt's concern with causes normally associated with the radical movement of his day, the *Examiner*'s values were related closely to his middle class orientation.[26] Hunt wrote, Carl Woodring demonstrates, "as an angry young bourgeois" repudiating the aristocratic assumption that it possesses a monopoly on "valor, probity, taste, and creative talent."[27] Hunt's was the voice of the most idealistic side of the middle class, the voice of its social and cultural potential. The "liberality of opinion"[28] that Hunt hoped to encourage in the growing middle ranges of English society he saw thwarted by the "lawless old gentleman" of the political establishment "to whom . . . human nature is an estate in fee," a position he later argued in the *Liberal*.[29] Because political leaders had not yet begun "the cultivation of the human intellect," the *Examiner* was necessary.

With Hunt's journal, he hoped to convince all who would listen of the need to apply philosophy—in its original sense, as the "love of wisdom"—to political thought since the "essence of philosophy is the cultivation of common reason."[30] "Freedom from party spirit," a condition essential in Hunt's view for political morality, "is nothing but the love of looking abroad upon men and things, and this leads to universality, which is the great study of philosophy, so that the true love of inquiry and the love of one's country move in a circle."[31] If these ideas—essentially an expression of Romantic Humanism—seem innocent enough now, they appeared very dangerous indeed in the early years of the Regency; therefore, publishing such concepts in the *Examiner* was an act of courage.

Reaction to the Napoleonic wars and earlier to the revolutions in America and in France had considerably diminished England's traditional freedoms.[32] Since conservative reaction carried the day, the exponents of reform, however justified, were suspect. Bent on suppressing what was viewed as a genuine radical threat to the country, Hunt's ministerial enemies classed him among such recognized opposition journalists and editors as William Hone, Richard Carlile, Thomas Wooler, and, of course, the infamous William Cobbett.[33] Naturally, the coincidence in the names of the radical "Orator Henry Hunt" and "Examiner Hunt" led to some genuine mistakes and to many deliberate associations meant to discredit Leigh. Along with such journals as the *Champion* and the *Register*, the *Examiner* opposed what it saw as the partisan dishonesty and genuine treason of establishment journals like the *Morning Post* and the *Courier*. In actual fact, though the *Examiner* shared a number of beliefs with this small, persecuted but vigorous segment of the press, it was typically more reasonable and its excesses fewer.

Hunt was never to become either a radical democrat or an antimonarchist. Although some critics speak with superior amusement of Hunt's vigorous denial late in life that he had ever opposed the monarchy,[34] he argued even in 1810 that genuine Whigs "were for monarchy but not for tyranny, for nobles but not for monopoly, for the people but not for licentiousness."[35] Like his often misunderstood friend Shelley, Hunt was more a reformer than revolutionary; for it was not the system but its evils that he attacked. Hence his enthusiasm for Jeremy Bentham (Hunt was one of his earliest journalistic supporters), Robert Owen, Sir Francis Burdett, Lord Brougham, and Sir Samuel Romilly resulted from their dedication to the principle of reform.[36] Although it is doubtful that Hunt ever completely understood any of these men, he saw political and social opinions he admired in each of them. As a "Constitutional meliorist,"[37] Hunt entered the battle wherever he found it joined, but he made neither public nor permanent alliances with these voices of change. Just as Hunt's literary criticism provides a sort of Romantic common denominator, so in matters of social thought his eclecticism produces a partial cross section of moderate liberal thought.

An idealist certainly, an idle dreamer rarely, Hunt concerned himself largely in these early years with specific issues rather than abstract schemes. He opposed theories of racial superiority and any form of slavery. He advocated both a considerable enlargement of the voting franchise and the reorganization of parliamentary seats to achieve greater fairness in representation. He sponsored military reform not just on humanitarian grounds but also from his patriotic desire to see England strong. He attacked, in addition to the Prince Regent, both Lord Castlereagh and the Duke of Wellington—the first one for political immorality; the second, for military excesses. In all men of power and authority he probed for consistent moral integrity, for he insisted that a man's behavior could not be compartmentalized. Never advocating or supporting Napoleon, Hunt made himself hated by many for recognizing the dishonor on both sides in the Napoleonic wars.

Hunt always argued in later years that he had actually forced himself of necessity to enter political controversies. Allowing for some exaggeration in this claim, we must recognize that the early *Examiner* years that culminated in his trial and imprisonment in 1813 marked the high tide of his involvement. After that point, his interest flagged considerably; but the change was not because he had been frightened into silence—on occasion the old fire would return to his now infrequent denunciations—but because his interests had simply shifted. In 1822, the *Liberal* seemed to represent a reawakened interest; for the preface to that remarkable journal contains much of the old *Examiner*'s vigor and enthusiasm for battle. Although the controlled beat of the preface represents Hunt at his best, he had clearly altered the entire basis for commentary: "The object of our work is not political, except inasmuch as all writing now-a-days must involve something to that effect, the connection between politics and all other subjects of interest to mankind having been discovered, never again to be done away."[38]

The *Liberal* would therefore invoke such men as Chaucer and Milton, indeed "all who have thrown light and life upon man, instead of darkness and death."[39] But this new literary orientation retained the old foundations; it saw man—"a being progressive, instead of a creeping creature retrograde"—deserving and gradually achieving freedom.[40] Moreover, if by 1832 Hunt had left the field altogether, to frequent instead the gentler realm of the familiar essay and the pleasure grounds of poetry, he had already served his purpose. As R. B. Johnson states, "the energy and fearlessness of his editorial utterances and the consistent vigour of his paper did no little service to the cause of Liberalism in one of its darkest periods."[41] Hunt had lived to see the success of most of his eminently humane and just causes.

## IV  *Literary Periodicals*

Although the *Examiner* made Hunt famous as a political commentator it was only the first of his numerous journals; moreover, to many, the enduring significance of this publication is not political but literary. Although preceded by two similar journals, Hunt's *Examiner* established a journalistic form to be followed generally for another fifty years and beyond.[42] In retrospect, Hunt placed great emphasis on the *Examiner*'s dedication to "the green places of poetry," and its literary orientation is obvious.

It is worth noting, for instance, that the careers of the two great contemporary essayists—Hazlitt and Lamb—are inextricably bound to the story of the *Examiner* and the *Reflector*. Hunt was one of the first to recognize and encourage Hazlitt's genius; and, as Baker says, the publication of his essays enabled Hazlitt, largely unknown at the time he joined the *Examiner* in 1815, "to make a reputation."[43] Hunt also gave the slightly better-known Lamb the room he needed to develop his characteristic style.[44] In a detailed study of the Romantic familiar essay, Marie Law credits Hunt's employment of these two authors, along with his own efforts, for the nurture and development of that form in the nineteenth century.[45] Later Hunt was to publish other important authors; in the *Tatler,* for instance, we find the work of Barry Cornwall; in the *Monthly Repository,* essays by Walter Savage Landor.

If this assistance to English letters was not enough, we have also Hunt's even more significant "discovery" of Keats and Shelley. "No literary editor," says one Shelley scholar, "is likely to make so famous a catch again."[46] Lamb and Hazlitt would have become great essayists without Hunt, but his friendship, encouragement, and publication of their work helped. The case is similar with Keats and Shelley; they received, if not essential aid, at least very useful assistance and considerable moral support from a published author and a well-known editor whose opinions they respected. It is fashionable among some literary historians to suggest that Hunt damaged rather than enhanced their reputations and to assume, of course, that the totally unknown Keats and the already criticized Shelley would otherwise have had an easy road to popularity, which assuredly would not have been the case.

Such a view also ignores the great influence Hunt's opinions had among the sensitive, intelligent, dissatisfied young men of the age. Keats first experienced the heady sweetness of publication when Hunt printed his sonnet "O Solitude! if I must with thee dwell" in the *Examiner* (May 5, 1816); thereafter, he found himself encouraged and treated seriously in the same journal, his poems quoted, and his fame predicted. Hunt printed a number of Shelley's poems from time to time, including "Hymn to Intellectual Beauty," "Ozymandius," and "To a Skylark." In Hunt's now famous *Examiner* essay "Young Poets," of December 1, 1816, about Keats, Shelley, and the forgotten John Hamilton Reynolds, Hunt began in earnest a campaign on behalf of the greater pair, that ended only with his death. And, since Hunt also initially supported the young Byron, the *Examiner* can surely be said to have been the most vigorous and articulate champion of the second generation of Romantic poets.

In the many journals that Hunt was to produce over the years, his preoccupation with literature manifested itself at times in the form of transient poetry, as well as in what he called "a sort of literary chit-chat."[47] But despite this "literary pocket-book" strain, he soon developed and demonstrated a firm conviction of the need for sound, illustrative periodical criticism. He had contempt for much of what passed for that kind of writing—its pretentiousness, its ludicrous detail, and its pedantry. His own approach to the critical essay early assumed its characteristic shape. The charming emblem for the *Indicator*—the indicator bird leading the seeker to the honey in the woods—symbolizes exactly his desire to present the reader with the experience of the work itself, rather than with his own esoteric and ingenious notions. His twin tools were tastefulness and shrewdness in sampling. He quoted copiously, for he assumed that, where he was wrong in his generalizations, the work itself would correct his errors. The resultant essays achieve a high degree of success in suggesting the essence of an artist's work. This "signpost criticism," as Johnson calls it,[48] was the result of his habitual desire to share the very best with his readers. He was not interested in criticism as an exercise in itself; he wished to find for deserving authors an appreciative audience and to help the largest possible audience find good writers.

### V *Journalist as Educator: "A Sense of What Their Nature Requires"*

Hunt's pronounced swing from politics to poetics clearly represents not simply a retreat into personal interest but a shift in the area of public service. As a reformer, Hunt wished to fill not only the stomachs of England's deserving poor but also their minds and souls; moreover, he knew there were many whose poverty was not at all physical. To inculcate the love of beauty or, on a less elevated level, to foster taste, was to him the duty of one who himself enjoyed it. This conviction is the basis for Hunt's compulsion to share. If his early career was devoted to political necessities, his middle and later years were continually dedicated to mental and spiritual education—to the well-being of the whole man. Marie Law believes that in his desire to bring beauty into all men's lives Hunt "anticipated Ruskin and William Morris."[49]

An esthetic democrat, Hunt was in fact a sort of one man national extension service. He wrote on behalf of literature, the theater, music, the plastic arts—always in hope of increasing popular appreciation. Recognizing that, in Hazlitt's words, "knowledge is no longer confined to the few" and that the time had come "to make it accessible and attractive to the many,"[50] Hunt threw his modest talents into the fight for educational and esthetic equality with the same gusto that had characterized his war against the regent. The great bulk of his efforts, spread over a long career, made Hunt, as Johnson reminds us, "a part of the great educational movements that were so closely associated with the liberal progress of the century."[51] The bourgeois center that we have observed in his political thought was paralleled by what amounts to missionary zeal, despite his casual methods, about education.

Hunt had received a useful education at Christ's Hospital, and in neither birth nor deportment did he deserve his enemies' label "cockney"; but neither was he a gentleman graduate of one of England's great universities. His loyalties were primarily with the burgeoning middle class and with those of the lower classes whose potential taste and creativity deserved to be encouraged. Keats may be taken as a perfect example; his lack of a traditional education did not prevent him from developing his genius. Hunt's introductions, illustrations, analyses, and samples were intended for people like Keats, whether they were writers or readers.

Perhaps the most openly educational in intent of Hunt's periodicals was one of the last, the *London Journal*; however, its philosophy, so clearly stated in the preface, actually characterizes his entire career. Its motto—"to assist the enquiring, animate the struggling, and sympathize with all"—nicely indicates the spirit of both his political and nonpolitical efforts. The preface assumes that the constructive forces of literature had already been felt and that it was his duty to encourage them. Even rural cottagers, he felt, "not withstanding their inferior opportunities, have caught from stray pieces of poetry and fiction, a sense of what their nature requires, in order to elevate its enjoyments or to console its struggles."[52] This clear statement indicates Hunt's tenacious faith in the higher purposefulness or "function" of art as a key to man's spiritual development—"what his nature requires"—and it is not simply a recognition of the recreational or decorative values of art, which, of course, he also acknowledges.

Because of Hunt's attitude, "the *London Journal* proposes to furnish ingenious minds of all classes, with such helps as it possesses towards a share in the pleasures of taste and scholarship."[53] Because "Man has not yet learnt to enjoy the world he lives in"[54] and because, like Descartes, Hunt equates life with consciousness of it, he offers heightened awareness and hence intensified life as the goal of his journal: the more the reader "knows, the more he exists; and the pleasanter his knowledge, the happier his existence."[55] By that token, "pleasure is the business of this Journal"[56]

At its extreme, the Romantic Humanism displayed by Hunt has distinctly religious overtones and implies something of a crusade. The political campaigning of the *Examiner* years was replaced with fervent "Christianizing [of] public manners"; for Hunt's ambition was, as he tells us in 1834, "to be one of the sowers of good seed in places where it is not common" and to see "love enshrined as the only final teacher of all knowledge and advancement." To that end, he dedicated "these small chapels [essays] built for conventional persuasion."[57] He is, of course, as much Shelleyan as Christian in his doctrine of love.

This attitude represents Hunt's permanent concern with the educational growth of his fellow men and is not simply an old man's optimism. In his 1828 "Companion's Farewell to his Readers," an essentially dignified essay despite the potential for self-dramatization, Hunt's theme is his unshakable faith in man's progress, material and spiritual: "I cannot help thinking, among other guesses, that something divine in the universe is constantly urging the mind of man to come to this better condition; and I am certain that endeavour is good at all events, and that we can only lose in every way by the rust of a sordid acquiescence."[58] Hunt feared man's intellectual status quo; and, in this essay as elsewhere, he associated evil largely with ignorance.

## VI  "*Chronicle for Posterity*"

Popular journalism (Hunt once claimed to be "the father of the present penny and three half-penny literature"[59]) had another task to perform in addition to extending "an acquaintance with matters of intellectual refinement among the uneducated."[60] As early as the prospectus to the *Reflector*, Hunt believed that magazines were responsible for recording the "*character of the times*"; and, since this activity was most important, all trivia was to be avoided so that the journal could assume its proper role as a "*Chronicle for posterity.*"[61] He would be, therefore, not only society's educator but also its historian.

It is unnecessary, however, to demonstrate how often the bulk of Hunt's periodical writing failed to devote itself, in any pure sense, to this high task. The *Examiner* does offer one of the most exciting if biased records of the early Regency; it throbs with the political and social issues with which active men were involved. But, after the early *Examiner* days, Hunt more and more turned to the personal essay; and he wrote such essays to wage his continual battle to win the world for art. The familiar essay, in many ways the prose equivalent of Romantic self-revelation in the lyric, became more and more the chief substance of his periodicals. Even the above noted offer of educational assistance in the *London Journal* was based on Hunt's claim that "there is scarcely a single joy or sorrow within the experience of our fellow-creatures which we have not tasted," and, by implication, were willing to share.[62] Johnson concluded that the failure of the *London Journal* resulted from Hunt's having been too subjective, too little concerned with the public events that had once so preoccupied him.[63] Yet much of his best writing resulted from such a charming myopia; and if his essays do compose a chronicle, they record half a century as seen through his eyes. And, as Priestly has observed, Hunt's strong journalistic bias results in his closer attention to the passing scene that we also find in the work of his great colleagues in the essay: many of his pieces "are like little peep-holes through which we may catch a vivid glimpse of the life of the Regency"[64] and, we may add, the growth of Victorian England.

Not surprisingly, Hunt's many personal essays also make the best introduction to the quality, if not the details, of his life; they counter his strange diffidence in his autobiography. Moreover, his literary as opposed to historical significance rests largely on his warm and personable familiar essays. In these works his temperament and journalistic values cause him continually to seek ways to reduce the distance between himself and his reader. This desire accounts in large part for the nature of his prose style.

## VII    *Prose Style*

In an excellent introduction to Hunt's autobiography, Morpurgo has reminded us of the need to weigh him "as a journalist" or even as a "hack" but "not as a man of letters."[65] Hunt recognized, even in his youthful vanity of 1807, that "Newspapers are not celebrated for their lasting materials"; and he was cheerfully "prepared to die" with the rest of his "transitory brethren . . . like a true gazetteer."[66] Considering Hunt's vast and uneven output, the size of his organizational units, and the journalistic medium in which he chose to work, Morpurgo's claim seems fair. But we should at once note the essentially literary quality of Hunt's prose and distinguish it from the artless, barely functional, and often tasteless writing that we frequently associate with journalism today. In Hunt's time, the line between the journalist and the author was quite indistinct; and, in his own case, it was nonexistent. Moreover, the general quality of his periodical writing was surprisingly high, considering its bulk.

To improve the standards of such writing was Hunt's constant effort, however, and we find him frequently citing and condemning badness in magazine writing.[67] The preface to Volume I of the *Examiner* lists two goals: first, the encouragement of independent thinking; second, "an attempt to improve the style of what is called fugitive writing, by setting an example of, at least, a *diligent respect for the opinion of literary readers.*"[68] He was particularly concerned with what he saw as a parallel between bad political prose and the immoral politics for which it was employed.[69] He understood the limitation of journalism, for he recognized that periodical writers could not compose for immortality. It was absurd in matters of style, he acknowledged, for a journalist "to promise that which haste or head-ache might hinder from performing."[70] Problems of necessary speed, lack of choice in subject matter, and lack of opportunities for revision—all these affected the journalist's level of performance.

But Hunt also recognized the significance of journalism's total impact on society, as well as its potential for raising the cultural level of general readers. His contribution to the press was good taste and general competence, and Bernbaum is not too generous when he claims that "Hunt's idealistic and scholarly standards helped to make journalism respectable."[71]

In regard to Hunt's respected prose, the influences upon it were neither unusual nor far to seek. His grammar school, Christ's Hospital, was a conservative institution; for his tutors the *Spectator* remained the established standard of style. And, if his school essays were so bad that they were often crumpled and thrown to other students by the terrible Boyer who would say " 'here, children, there is something to amuse you,' "[72] the final result was Hunt's acceptance of high literary standards for "fugitive writing." Of the two great Augustan essayists, Hunt preferred "Steele with all his faults, to Addison with all his essays."[73] In a set of British classics given him by his father, Hunt discovered the *Connoisseur* of the elder Colman and Bonnell Thornton, a periodical that had run for one hundred and forty numbers between 1754 - 1756. These essays in the mode of the *Tatler* and *Spectator* gave him, he said, "an entirely fresh and delightful sense of the merits of essay writing," and he felt a bond of sympathy between these more accessible models

and his own impulse toward "anti-formalities."[74] When the chance
came in 1804 for Hunt to write for Quin's *Traveler*, he borrowed
the signature "Mr. Town, Critic and Censor-general" from the
*Connoisseur;* but he added "junior" to indicate his appren-
ticeship.[75]

Despite Hunt's "anti-formalities" (which eventually produced a
most un-neo-Classical style), the other great influence on his early
prose was the still vigorous legacy of Dr. Johnson. We have only to
dip into any of Hunt's introductions to his five volume edition of
*Classic Tales* (1806 - 1807) to find not only Johnson's critical
vocabulary but also his rhetoric, one often imitated with laborious
artificiality. And, at the outset of the *Examiner* ("On Periodical
Essays"), Hunt invokes Johnson and Addison among others. Then
in their spirit he rolls forth his own period: "If I can persuade the
public to hear me after these celebrated men, I shall think myself
extremely fortunate; if I can amuse them with any originality, I
shall think myself deserving; if I procure them any moral benefit, I
shall think myself most happy."[76]

But the "attractive and the unaffected" quality with which Hunt
had already credited Goldsmith over the greater Swift and Johnson
in *Classic Tales*[77] was more nearly akin to Hunt's own vivacious and
casual temperament than were the sterner elements in these great
predecessors. The time was one of transition in prose style, moreover, a transition that Hunt assisted both as a writer and as an
editor. Although it was inevitable that the young Hunt imitated the
more obvious elements of Johnson's style, it was also inevitable that
he should eventually break with that tradition. Except for an initial
pompous audacity resulting from Hunt's youthful overconfidence,
almost nothing in his personality responded to the formal rhetoric of
the past. His temperament—cheerful, warm, impulsive—lent itself
to a more natural and spontaneous style than older complexity
would permit. He wrote rapidly and copiously, not only because of
journalistic demands but because of a fluency so pronounced as
nearly to be his undoing. George Saintsbury thought Hunt became
"no contemptible master of this middle style"; for, despite Hunt's
composition speed and volume, he never fell into the tawdriness
and slovenliness of "penny-a-lining."[78] And, although his prose is
often marked by a mild looseness, it is never unpleasantly slack; and
it is nearly always clear and energetic. Moreover, there is a graceful
ease in his work, the result perhaps of a mind concerned with the
simply human rather than with rare and clotted abstractions.

The essential characteristic of Hunt's prose style is its strong colloquial quality; everywhere his better work creates the impression of the conversation of a man with the leisure to talk. Describing the contrast between the *Examiner* and the *Indicator*, Hunt explained that, in the former, he had "a sort of public meeting with his friends: in the other, a more retired one." In short, he opposed the "tavern-room" to "the study";[79] but he argued against any essential distinction between writing and speaking. As early as *Classic Tales* (where he least fulfills the description), he argued that "an author after all merely talks to his reader by signs instead of speech; and therefore the most perfect style seems to be that which avoids the negligence while it preserves the spirit of conversation."[80] But Hunt did not always avoid the negligence; for some "chatty" or even "gossipy" pieces cease to be artistic. But such moments are often saved by his essential humility; he is more likely to offend through occasional pretentiousness when reaching for profundity and a more elevated style.

He knew that the personal voice was his forte; that, although more esthetically conservative readers were offended by his intimacy, the bulk of his audience enjoyed the rejection of authorial distance. In addition to discarding the style of the great eighteenth century essayists, Hunt soon put aside the typical persona—a significant event in the development of the familiar essay.[81] "I speak all in my own name and at my own risk, whereas the custom is to rail and play the hypocrite in a mask," Hunt claims in an autobiographical sketch originally intended for *Lord Byron and Some of His Contemporaries;* similarly, in the first number of the "Wishing-Cap" papers, Hunt argues that it is impossible for him to employ a fictitious character like Bickerstaff.[82] Perhaps only Hunt would have written an essay in which he expressed concern about the implications of "I and we." He admits being "very much hampered with this *I* of mine," but he finds the editorial "we" unnatural, like one who says "we got a bruise on our knee." He asserts that "I have been accustomed to chat with the readers of the *Examiner* so long and so familiarly that I feel present, as of old, at their breakfasts and fireside."[83]

Like other literary genres during the Romantic period, the familiar essay had become a vehicle for self-revelation. Faith in the imagination, the debate over the necessity for rhyme and verse in poetry, the general subjectivity of art—all these tended to blur the traditional distinctions between poetry and prose. Not surprisingly, as Marie Law points out, Romantic essayists such as Hunt began to "interpret life subjectively, not in a metaphysical and reasoning manner, but in an imaginative and intuitive manner, analogous to that of the poet."[84] Hunt usually demanded that poetry possess "the fit sculpture of verse"; but, when unable to write the poem itself, he found prose a satisfying, if unequal, substitute. The following passage from "Dreams on the Borders of the Land of Poetry" suggests this idea:

But I have the wish to be a poet, and thoughts will arise within me as painful not to express as a lover's. I therefore write memorandums for verse;—thoughts that might perhaps be worthy of putting into that shape if they could be properly developed;—hints and shadows of something poetical, that have the same relationship to actual poetry as the little unborn spirits that perish by the waters of Lethe have to the souls that visit us, and become immortal.[85]

However, while being obviously self-aware, Hunt is almost never deeply self-analytical, even in his *Autobiography* or in his autobiographical essays. Hence, rather than becoming the subject of his own essays, his peculiar sensibility plays ceaselessly over the surface of life and gives his work its uniquely personal quality. Moreover, the direction of his interest is always outward toward experience shared with his reader. Possessing a kind of Wordsworthian sense of memory's significance—"vivid personal recollections, especially in solitude, produce a strong sense of one's individuality"[86]—he nonetheless employs the fruit of that memory to illuminate common, universal experiences. Thus, although his personality appears constantly in his work and although the very details of his daily life provide the material for many of his essays, he is never selfishly egotistical. Once again, he is motivated by a desire to share.

Like Montaigne (with whom Hunt has been favorably compared),[87] Hunt shared his talents and personality freely. His essential gift, which even in our own skeptical age appears genuine, was a temperamental and philosophical cheerfulness that was largely derived from his ability to find beauty, wonder, and joy in ordinary as well as in extraordinary things. His interest in all aspects of life was tremendous, and the sheer enjoyment he experienced in observation was far greater than that of most men. Thus, "whereas the eighteenth-century essayist is usually concerned to point a moral," Jack suggests, "Hunt's aim is to communicate enjoyment."[88]

VIII   *Essayist: "Cherry-Stone Workmanship"*

Early in Hunt's career as a student of other writers' work, he described Goldsmith as a writer who "does not appear to have possessed an attention sufficiently persevering to pursue one individual subject through a long maze of reasoning. Hence he was fond of detached essays, into which he could throw the result of his meditation and experience without tiring himself or his readers."[89] We could not desire a more accurate description of Hunt himself, for he was most comfortable with the small, unsustained unit. Even his books, it may be argued, are actually collections of these units cemented together by some common theme. Hunt referred to his own essays as a kind of "cherry-stone workmanship,"[90] an apt enough description if we are thinking, as he was, of scope and not of meticulous composition and organization. A born miscellanist, he was capable, as a good journalist must be, of writing short articles about a wide variety of topics with little advance preparation and with perhaps only the slightest suggestion to develop. He found this kind of writing congenial; his full range of interests and his retentive mind allowed him to promise to "take up . . . any subject to which I feel an impulse."[91] The subjects include people (living or dead, real or imaginary), places, things, activities, nature, and, of course, literature. A sort of generic mind informs these essays.

In these essays, as elsewhere in Hunt's work, shifting literary tastes and preferences damaged his reputation. We do not so highly value the essay as did the nineteenth century because we overemphasize its perishable nature; for, since we are accustomed to modern subliterary and purely utilitarian journalism, we do not anticipate or appreciate the wealth of imaginative life it may possess. Although we could read the *Examiner* to gain some understanding of Regency political broils, or Hunt's literary essays for a contemporary view of letters and for some understanding of the nature and quality of criticism in the period, many of Hunt's essays can be read only for the entertainment they often, even usually, provide. Our preparation for these essays simply involves accepting nonfunctional writing. In browsing through Hunt's periodicals, we are arrested by a curious title, read a few paragraphs, and then discover that the same kind of human contact and communication found in a fine conversation causes us to continue. We may possibly learn something—Hunt's frequent essays on the London scene, for instance, contain fascinating details about contemporary urban life—but our chief pleasure is in experiencing an imaginative mind's extension into prose.

Hunt's best familiar essays are found in the *Indicator* (1819-1821), the *Companion* (1828), and the *London Journal* (1834-1835); but we find fine pieces of the miscellaneous variety in all of his journals. He recognized his talent for these essays: "they tell me I am at my best at this work, which succeeds beyond all expectation."[92] And indeed they did tell him; Lamb, for example, claimed in a sonnet that the "flow . . . of brain" in these essays, the "observation, wit, and sense," suggested the return of Bickerstaff. His poem concludes with an accurate appraisal:

> The *Indicative* is your *Potential Mood*
> Wit, poet, prose-man, party-man, translator—
> H____, your best title yet is *Indicator*.[93]

These essays typically possess exactly the easy flow of mind of which Lamb speaks; they are gentle, bright, kindly, and always intelligent.

Not surprisingly, Hunt's friends had favorite essays—ones appropriate to their individual tastes. Lamb admired "Coaches and their Horses," "Thoughts and Guesses on Human Nature," and "Deaths of Little Children," a sort of "valediction forbidding mourning" that consists of folk wisdom pertaining to grief. Hazlitt preferred "A Few Thoughts on Sleep," "an article for the reader to think of, when he or she is warm in bed, a little before he goes to sleep, the clothes at his ear, and the wind moaning in some distant crevice."[94] Shelley liked best "The Fair Revenge," no doubt because of the heroine's submissive love and the pathos of two ruined lives that are the result of one hardened heart. Keats chose "A Now, Description of a Hot Day," a little study of English hot weather that describes slightly exaggerated but typical conditions: dusty roads, thirsty men, loosened bodices, and, finally, "the author, who has a plate of strawberries brought him, finds that he has come to the end of his writing." But he cannot conclude without mentioning those of his "numerous predecessors" who have employed this useful "now" so frequently. Hence he chooses to conclude with a passage from Beaumont and Fletcher's *The Woman Hater*; but, in locating it, he discovers it to be irrelevant to his theme. Undaunted, he quotes a page of dialogue, arguing that the passage "affords such an agreeable specimin of the wit and humour with which fine poets could rally the commonplaces of their art, that we cannot help proceeding with it."[95]

The conclusion of this last essay demonstrates something of the nature of tone and form in these conversational essays. The reader never knows what little discovery he will make in the next paragraph, for Hunt is perfectly willing to mix his subjects. Nor does he feel any obligation, as Priestly notes, "to deal with subjects only on one level, or to restrict the treatment to one 'key.' "[96] The medley is attractive, but the principle of unity must be found in the author's sensibility, not in the subject or in its treatment. In "Coaches and their Horses," the subject itself provides a loose framework; but the essay shifts in tone from gay to nostalgic to serious as the author's mind plays with his materials. We do not feel the essay to be disorganized; but, after a careful examination, we realize he planned neither where nor how he would end. In the earlier political essays, we rarely discover any formal rhetorical structure. These pieces were often triggered and given form by that which they were in reaction to, an editorial or a speech perhaps. And usually, as Woodring notes, Hunt's "political pieces best achieve organic unity when they center in a single emotion—indignation, the rare joy of a victory, or the anger of disappointment."[97] Often the *Indicator* type essay was intended by Hunt to be only a container or vehicle, as is the case with "The *Indicator* and *Examiner*.—Autumnal Commencement of Fires.—Mantle-Pieces.—Apartments for Study." Hunt opens by contrasting the two journals as "private room" and "tavern-room"; and, when he moves to attitudes toward weather in England and Italy, he links this discussion to the previous one by fires. The subject of fires leads to fireside activities such as reading and talking, to mantlepieces (by way of the writer's gaze falling upon an antique Athenian dish that his mantle supports), and to the question of which kind of room makes the best study, which appears to necessitate reference to Ariosto and Montaigne. When the "essay" concludes with two bits of poetry, the second seventeen lines comprise "a fine passionate burst of enthusiasm on the subject of a study in Fletcher's play of the Elder-Brother."[98] This piece, like many Romantic works, is organized on a purely associational basis; and we find a kind of subjective logic to the flow. This essay reads rather like a good letter from an engaging and affectionate friend.

In some cases, Hunt made deliberate use of the actual letter form as literary or journalistic strategy, a practice he inherited from the eighteenth century. Occasionally, the letter is used as a mask, as in some obviously bogus letters from and replies to his readers; at other times, it is a vehicle for social and literary commentary, as in his interesting "letters from abroad" series in the short-lived *Liberal*. Used to organize an essay, the epistolary form helps control fluctuations in tone, suggesting as it does a specific audience. But in Hunt's hands, the use of the epistle represents the rejection rather than the creation of a traditional persona; for the employment of this presentation is simply another way to capitalize on the personal basis of all his essays. Curiously enough, Hunt's private letters possess much less of the vivacity and graceful intimacy of his familiar essays. Although we find exceptions—for instance, his well-known letter to Joseph Severn written during the last days of Keats, and some letters to Shelley—Hunt's letters are disappointing, especially when compared with those of Lamb.

Two other uses to which Hunt put the essay deserve note—his tales and his character sketches. His tales depend not only upon our essential human curiosity but also on a particular story's power to transform a moment through the demonstration of some human potential. These are often retellings that make available experiences that Hunt feels to be in some way valuable and to be shared. The character sketches show not only the expected influence of seventeenth century work in this vein, as well as of Steele and Sterne, but also of Shenstone and, more particularly, Chaucer.[99] In these studies, Hunt is much stronger in the variety and appropriateness of his details than in his analytic depth. Yet in both the tales and the character sketches we feel Hunt to be on the edge of fiction.

As Baker says in *The History of the English Novel*, "this was a genre in which Leigh Hunt was shining; his studies of places and people . . . were in a manner as old as Goldsmith and as recent as Charles Lamb, but more circumstantial in their local colour and more personal and sociable in their human features, more free and easy and at the same time more trivial. They often approached the novel, sometimes more than half-way. The likeness of Boz to Leigh Hunt in the *Sketches* is close and obvious."[100] Indeed, critics have long since recognized that Dickens used Hunt's essays, among those of other great essayists, as models; and we wonder why Hunt did not himself write fiction since his greatest potential seemed to lie in that direction. That he had the opportunity is clear, for the publishers of Dickens' *Pickwick Papers* had originally considered Hunt to provide the text for their illustrator.

A glance at Hunt's single genuine attempt at fiction suggests one answer. His three volume novel, *Sir Ralph Esher* (1832), fails to transcend Hunt's nonfictional interests. In it Hunt utilizes his considerable antiquarian knowledge of the Restoration, his interest in the literature of that era, and his fascination with old London. To a large extent, he is successful in exploiting these interests; but he has little of what Keats called "negative capability." Consequently, none of his characters come alive, not even Sir Philip Herne who, as a manuscript annotation in Hunt's hand indicates, was modeled after Shelley. Dickens went beyond sketches, beyond accurate detail, to realize the living personality. Hunt was too concerned with the "sentiment elevating to the human heart and its hopes" that he saw as a necessary element in fiction.[101] The very use of the deeply admired Shelley as hero suggests a strong didactic motive.

But we find a simpler, more basic reason why Hunt did not develop his talents for fiction writing: he had almost no ambition in this direction. His nonjournalistic energies were largely devoted to the beloved poetry. Moreover, both the scope and the need to exercise authorial distance alienated him. It is significant that *Sir Ralph Esher* was written not as the result of Hunt's spontaneous choice, but rather at the request of his publisher Colburn, whose interest was commercial. In the main, this novel reflects Hunt as the indefatigable bookmaker, not as a potential Victorian novelist. Despite his failures to animate his characters, the novel is at least as good as Scott's *Woodstock*, written about the period preceding that portrayed by Hunt, and full of wooden references to "Will" Shakespeare and his fellow Renaissance playwrights.

## IX  *Editor and Anthologist*

When Hunt was not writing for his own or someone else's journals, he was making books. In addition to his many individual and collected volumes of poetry and essays; his books on theater, religion, and politics; and his editions of several older authors; Hunt compiled more than a dozen anthologies of poetry, essays, and tales from his own and other authors' works. During the 1840s alone, he produced nine such volumes in six years, not counting other literary efforts. By this time, he was a dean of letters, skilled at editing, at writing introductions, and at annotating. But his habit of making books had started early, with a collection of *Classic Tales* in 1806-1807; and this preoccupation lasted throughout his life. Following his death, several more compilations appeared, notably his *Book of the Sonnet* in 1867.

Hunt was probably tempted by the ease and economics of such

work. His wide range of knowledge and interests, his talent for pertinent generalization, and his faculty for fast, graceful prose may have encouraged him to produce some volumes of dubious value. For instance, Keats properly objected to Hunt's *The Literary Pocket Book,* an annual edited in 1819 to 1823 that contained a sort of culture kit of addresses of authors, museums, and so forth that were tied together by somewhat affected editorial tissue. There were also what Johnson has called "the counter-sweepings of a voluminous journalist,"[102] such as Hunt's *Table Talk* (1851).

This last objection might be made against *Men, Women, and Books* (1847), a volume of his previously uncollected essays originally published in such respectable journals as the *Edinburgh Review.* However, such books helped feed a growing appetite for reading material among the newly literate classes and among those members of the burgeoning middle class who were only then availing themselves of literary and cultural possibilities. Since Hunt was not snobbish, since he was ambitious about the printed work, and since he looked everywhere for readers, it is not surprising that he edited probably the first commuter literature, *Readings for Railways* (1849). This pocket-sized miscellany consists of tales, poetry, useful information, and other odds and ends that range from "Effects of Railway Velocity on Sound" to "Early Literature of Iceland." Hunt's frank sales appeal opens *A Jar of Honey from Mount Hybla* (1847), his disciplined collection of literary, historical, social, and mythological observations about Sicily and related subjects. Its introduction is preceded by "Christmas in Italy," "a modest essay showing the extreme fitness of this book for the season." Despite this self-advertisement, *Jar of Honey* is one of Hunt's most charming and successful bookmaking ventures. Among its twelve chapters (including one actually on bees), we have interesting discussions of Theocritus, as well as of the Italian and English pastoral. The final fourth of this little volume is devoted to a characteristic Huntian device, nine short "overflowings of the jar," interesting odds and ends that include Moschus' "Elegy on the Death of Bion" and that conclude with a short description of an Anglo-Sicilian Christmas dinner.

But the impression should not be left that all of these projects cost him little or no effort. Hunt wrote most of *Jar of Honey* himself; in other cases, he usually supplied an extensive editorial apparatus. *Imagination and Fancy* (1844) and *Wit and Humour* (1846), two volumes of a projected five volume categorical anthology of "none but genuine poetry," were each provided with seventy page critical introductions as well as with lengthy headnotes. Editing the two volume *Stories From the Italian Poets* (1846) required Hunt to survey the works of five writers—Dante, Pulci, Boiardo, Ariosto, and Tasso—and to translate and then render into prose each of his selections. Moreover, the edition includes elaborate critical and biographical notes, occasional verse translations paired with the originals, and an abstract of Dante's entire work.

Behind Hunt's editorial selections in all his anthologies of literature was the desire to introduce the reader to good things he himself had enjoyed, to share the results of his own wide, sympathetic reading of authors new and old. No editor trusted more fully in his own taste. The anthologizer has the right, he argued in the preface to *A Book For a Corner* (1849), "to boast of his originals, especially when they are such as have comforted and delighted him throughout his own life, and are for that reason recommended by him to others."[103] As this quotation shows, his taste leaned toward works providing spiritual solace or diversion; and either kind is frequently a species of escapism. During the period of Hunt's influence, Keats struggled with the need he felt to pass beyond the delights of "Flora, and Old Pan" to a poetry confronting "the agonies, the strife / Of human hearts," a struggle dramatized in his poem "Sleep and Poetry," written after a night spent in Hunt's study. Less troubled than his young friend by guilt stemming from a desire to escape "a sense of real things," Hunt would have accepted, without analyzing its latent paradox, Keats' argument in "Sleep and Poetry" that "the great end / Of poesy" is "To sooth the cares, and lift the thoughts of man," a doctrine Keats may well have absorbed from Hunt.

Consequently Hunt's anthologies are often slanted toward selections that contribute to the reader's peace of mind or pleasure as they had already done for the editor. In selecting poetry for *Imagination and Fancy*, for instance, Hunt is perfectly aware of the difference between his taste for Shakespeare's "fanciful scenes" rather than his tragic vision; but his anthology "is intended to give the reader no perplexity, except to know what to admire most."[104] In a *Book For a Corner*, the "perennials" have a comfortable unpretentiousness about them, and they lack any great passion or painfully complex insight. The collection is perhaps best characterized by Shenstone's "The Schoolmistress" and by Gray's "Elegy in a Country Churchyard" (that "quintessence of humanity"). [105] Reflecting his abiding desire to improve the minds and spirits of all, especially those of the middle class (whose taste he not only helped to shape but also shared), Hunt can only "hope many a man of business will refresh himself with the short pieces in these volumes, and return to his work the fitter to baffle craft, and yet retain a reverence for simplicity." [106] Not surprisingly, many of his selections are also characterized by "the greatest of all interests—domestic interest," [107] as Hunt claimed in his preface to *One Hundred Romances of Real Life* (1843).

Like other Romantic and Victorian poetry editors, Hunt displayed a clear preference for what Myer Abrams calls the "incandescent passage"; [108] and he was little concerned with questions of wholeness and unity. While *Imagination and Fancy* includes complete short poems, a great deal of space is given to extractions, often brief, from longer works. In part, this practice results from Hunt's fascination with small, intense moments of "pure poetry"; but he would not have accepted Edgar Allen Poe's argument against the possibility of the long poem. Other reasons for Hunt's fragmentation include his method of introduction by way of short samples, his interest in passages expressing powerfully a sentiment he shared, or, more typically, his preoccupation with style—metrics, for instance—as opposed to content.

If we think that these editorial practices appear limiting, we should also recognize that whatever Hunt's motive was in making a selection, he almost always demanded that the piece justify itself esthetically. A specific kind but the best of its kind might summarize or express his motto. The feast that Hunt served is generally light and on the sweet side, yet unquestionably delicious. If the reader of Hunt's selections is denied the spiritual reaches of a tragic ascent, he is at least rewarded with fine examples of less passionate or disturbing literary pleasures. Moreover, in note after note, preface after preface, Hunt makes perfectly clear what merits justify a selection; he is as much concerned with developing the reader's basis for taste as he is with his appreciation of specific works. Making judicious selections for his readers is, he feels, a major responsibility of the literary critic—and to this important aspect of Hunt's career we now turn.

CHAPTER 5

# Literary Critic

## I  *Critic as Educator*

W E might actually argue that in a conventional sense
Hunt was not a critic, and that he did not aspire to become
one. For him, the most useful critical act was not primarily to
evaluate or to explicate; "he was," as Amy Lowell so accurately explained, "a great introducer."[1] In three issues of the *Tatler* (October 13, 14, 15, 1830), Hunt pursues a long discussion of "An
Analysis With Occasional Translation, of the Lutrin of Boileau,"
and in so doing demonstrates his critical motives and methods.
Despite the title, the article is really not an analysis, at least in the
modern sense. Rather, it is a kind of miniature anthology—literally
a breaking down into parts rather than an interpretation—of Hunt's
quite good translations of passages he thinks "fine" or crucial to an
appreciation of the poem; and these quotations are accompanied
by prose connections and summaries. He wishes "that the reader
may be as well acquainted with it as ourselves,"[2] and the opening
paragraph makes clear his goal: "From time to time . . . we shall
offer our readers . . . an account of an old poem, which though
famous to this country by name, and well known to persons with
French, has never yet had a reasonable taste given of it to that
numerous body of readers, who knowing no language but their
own, are yet capable of relishing the best works in any."[3]

Commonly unknown or unavailable literature is frequently central to Hunt's critical papers; and, in the case of this example, the
poem is both seldom read and (he mistakenly thinks) unavailable in
English. At least he can provide a "taste"; and, in so doing, he is
driven on by his chief critical motive—the education of the
audience. He is attempting, as he claims elsewhere, "to give the
English reader as universal a taste as possible of fine writers."[4] His

103

faith in the value of a popular culture explains his "analysis" of
Boileau's *Lutrin* and his insertion of minor Renaissance poems as
"filler" elsewhere in his journal; in many ways, Hunt, not
Wordsworth, was the democrat of the arts. Moreover, Hunt desired
to bring people in contact not only with literature, music, and art
but with the whole world of intellectual exploration and discovery.
He saw literature as an inclusive category; for those readers—and
he hoped they were many—who "are desirous of becoming acquainted with anything that concerns mankind at large" even
politics may be seen as "a part of humane literature."[5] This broader
view accounts for the motto given his *London Journal:* "To assist
the inquiring, animate the struggling, and sympathize with all."

To Hunt, good critics are "those who have thought and felt" for
the reader, and who, because of their "trustworthiness" and their
"good-humour,"[6] are accepted by those whom they would educate.
But, as an educator, Hunt never assumed a pedantic role; he wrote
as an intimate, and his articles often sound more like letters to a
friend than formal discussions. He saw himself as "chatting comfortably"[7] with his reader, not lecturing him. In the preface to
*Imagination and Fancy,* he informs readers that his method of commentary is based on the "*principle of co-perusal,* as though the
Editor were reading the passages in their company."[8] In the preface
to *Wit and Humour,* Hunt explains his considerable use of italics as
originating "in a wish expressed by the readers of a periodical work,
who liked the companionship which it implied between reader and
editor."[9] He can be described, in short, with Wordsworth's definition of the poet,—"a man speaking to men."

Hunt's view of the critic as one who genially shares his own
cultural experiences with his lesser privileged readers has added
significance when we realize the breadth of his taste. In 1841, when
Hunt had largely outlived his earlier detractors, Macaulay found in
him "what is very rare in our time, the power of justly appreciating
and heartily enjoying good things of very different kinds."[10]
Saintsbury later described Hunt as being "perhaps more *catholic* in
his tastes as regards English Literature than any critic up to his
time."[11] Despite Hunt's early Romantic repudiation of the "French
School," he never really denied any English literary period. Beyond
England, he carried his readers far and wide in time and space: to
the Classics, to literature of the European Middle Ages, and to
literature of contemporary Europe.

As a translator and as a critic, Hunt claimed to "read closely and with a due sense of what the poet demands";[12] and such care made him a valuable guide to his readers. Moreover, he had an open mind; he was willing to be persuaded by the critical care and judgment of others. In the *London Journal* for July and August of 1834, he discussed "Specimens of Celebrated Authors," featuring Goethe; and, as usual, Hunt hoped to provide the reader with "a taste of the man himself."[13] Between the writing of numbers eighteen and nineteen for the *Journal*, he read various criticisms of Goethe, especially Carlyle's "Characteristics"; and in number nineteen he is prepared to react again with more of his own comments. After still more exposure to Carlyle's analysis, Hunt relinquishes his earlier, negative reactions; admits his own kindling enthusiasm; and concludes with more extracts from the great German's work. As a result of experience, he formulated opinion; and new experience led to new opinion. When he was challenged by a good critic, his honesty forced him to modify his convictions concerning a topic that he had thought he understood; and others could profit from his careful response to literature.

In "Ultra-Germano-Criticasterism," a little squib Hunt aimed at bad critics, he attacks critical subjectivity (to "palm your own creed" on the reader) and especially intellectual pretentiousness. But, generally, his greatest scorn was for the small-minded, often nasty critic. Writing in the *Tatler* in 1831, Hunt evaluated contemporary critics and criticism in a strikingly negative manner: "The truth is, that criticism itself, for the most part, is a nuisance and an impertinence: and no good-natured, reflecting men would be critics, if it were not that there are worse. . . . Critics, for the most part, are not of the first order of literati, otherwise they would be better occupied: they are often of the very worst order, and therefore are perniciously occupied."[14] Because of such convictions, Hunt pledges to be an "honest but not ill-natured critic" and hopes "to furnish the reader with such glimpses into the regions of pleasant and improving thoughts as experience may have helped us to."[15] The assumption is his usual one: that a wider distribution of art and intellectual inquiry will significantly assist in the evolution of a liberal, humane society.

Hunt held this motive in common with Shelley and the Romantic movement in general; and many would have approved the goal claimed for the *Tatler:* Our "object . . . is to assist in keeping humanity in heart and hope for the diviner times, which liberality is producing."[16] These lines, written in anticipation of England's 1832

reform bill, illustrate Hunt's modest but genuine faith in the
Romantic social apocalypse celebrated and rejected long before by
Wordsworth and Coleridge. Earlier, Hunt had gone to jail in support of his political convictions; by 1831, he had come to depend
upon education to achieve the long-awaited transformation.[17]

## II  *Romantic Theory: Imagination and Fancy*

Although we have emphasized Hunt's commitment to criticism as
education, he did not simply present and recommend; he also formulated general esthetic theories and provided some analysis and
evaluation based on them. We should acknowledge at the outset,
however, that Hunt's intellectual faculties for synthesis were not of
the first order and that he was not especially interested in
theoretical matters. He correctly recognized that his "faculty, such
as it is, is rather instinctive than reasoning";[18] and this distinction
reflects not only the Romantic apotheosis of the imagination but
also his awareness of his own temperament. Nonetheless, it is inac-
curate to conclude, as a number of scholars have, that his critical
successes were simply the result of intuitive fortuitousness; for Hunt
eventually possessed a considerable number of precepts (some con-
tradictory) that were bound together by his temperament and by a
sort of generalized contemporary attitude rather than any highly articulated system.

These principles are explicit or implicit everywhere throughout
the amazing bulk of his critical writings; however, only in 1844,
many years after the high water mark of Romantic critical theory,
did he write any sustained thesis. This work is the seventy-five page
essay, "An Answer to the Question What is Poetry" that is the
preface of his anthology *Imagination and Fancy*. Along with a
similar preface to *Wit and Humour* (the only other anthology completed in a series to contain only "genuine poetry"[19]), this short but
very comprehensive work contains the essence of his critical principles. Four editions in Hunt's lifetime and four more before the
end of the century, as well as American editions, make this book
Hunt's most permanent contribution to Romantic poetic theory.

The temptation to compare Hunt's *Imagination and Fancy* with
Coleridge's *Biographia Literaria* of 1817 or with Wordsworth's
famous preface of 1800 has proved irresistible to most commen-
tators. The differences in quality are unmistakable, but Hunt's
motives and his position in regard to the theory he treats are very

different from those of his two great contemporaries. Wordsworth's preface to *Lyrical Ballads* was a revolutionary manifesto; innocuous as it may now seem, it was nothing less than the French Revolution of English literature, as Hazlitt recognized. Coleridge's *Biographia Literaria*, on the other hand, attempted both an inventory and the construction of an immensely sophisticated and complex philosophical analysis of what had come to be thought by the new men as the essence of poetry. Coleridge writes as an esthetician with a lofty goal; and his theory of poetry, he argued in *Biographia Literaria*, would "in its immediate effects furnish a torch of guidance to the philosophical critic; and ultimately to the poet himself."[20] Hunt's goal was to popularize; his audience was the public; and, if there is a general lowering of the level of complexity, at least the Romantic doctrine was available to the great new reading class, as in Coleridge it surely was not.

Indeed, Hunt was not one of the great formulators of Romantic esthetic theory. Rather, he was a kind of common denominator—a way to measure the widespread shift in critical orientation that had taken place in his lifetime. As Stephen Fogle so correctly states, Hunt's preface to *Imagination and Fancy* "is a summing-up and explanation, a charting of ground already won, rather than an attempt to explore the future."[21] In relationship to the critical canon Hunt expounds, his *Imagination and Fancy* is more like Pope's *Essay on Criticism* than Wordsworth's preface or Coleridge's literary biography. The differences between his essay and the greater tracts are evident in his statement of motives:

The object of the book is threefold;—to present the public with some of the finest passages in English poetry, *so marked and commented;*—to furnish such an account, in an Essay, of the nature and requirements of poetry, *as may enable readers in general to give an answer on those points to themselves and others;*—and to show, throughout the greater part of the volume, what sort of poetry is to be considered *as poetry of the most poetical kind,* or such as exhibit the imagination and fancy in a state of predominance, undisputed by interests of another sort.[22]

Like a good teacher, Hunt's guidance is intended to be "in no spirit of dictation to anyone."[23]

Hunt recognizes, in *Imagination and Fancy*, that "the critical distinction between Fancy and Imagination was hardly determined till of late," for Collins and Milton had used "the word Fancy to imply both" terms.[24] It is possible that Hunt is referring in this statement to Coleridge's declaration in the fourth chapter of *Biographia Literaria* "that fancy and imagination were two distinct and widely different faculties, instead of being, according to the general belief, either two names with one meaning, or at furthest the lower and higher degree of one and the same power."[25] It is more likely, however, that Hunt's reference is to the preface of Wordsworth's 1815 edition in which he attempts to justify his classifications "Poems of the Fancy" and "Poems of the Imagination." By the time of *Imagination and Fancy*, Hunt maintains the distinction; but, though he had used the terms long before Coleridge's famous distinction appeared, we can not ascertain just when Hunt recognized a clear difference in the function, if not in the nature, of fancy and imagination. He used imagination early and late to define the artist's vital faculty, but the term frequently appears alone and in the most general way. In fact, we find in Hunt's early work a jumble of traditional and contemporary critical terms. For instance, in 1815 he uses the mimetic term "mirror" and "imagination" (apparently in its modern sense) in the same sentence.[26] In *Classic Tales* (1806), "fancy" and "imagination" are used together but not necessarily in opposition. In an 1808 essay, we find in a brief space a cluster of terms having Romantic significance—"Fancies," "imagination," "inspiration," "enthusiasm," "insanity"—that are used very loosely.[27] In an 1811 article on Thomas Moore's *M. P.; Or, The Blue Stocking*, "fancy" and "imagination" appear to be the interchangeable terms that he found confused by Collins and Milton.[28]

In *Imagination and Fancy*, however, Hunt makes a clear distinction between the uses of the two faculties, though not initially. As a part of the amplification of his opening definition of poetry, the distinction is neither sharp nor altogether consistent with the more detailed later discussion. At the outset, poetry "embodies and illustrates its impressions by imagination, or images of the objects which it treats . . . in order that it may enjoy and impart the feeling of their truth in its utmost conviction and affluence." Fancy, which also "illustrates" those impressions, is seen as "a lighter play of imagination."[29]

Later in the essay Hunt begins to create a real distinction by deepening the significance of imagination and by underlining its immense importance in the creative act. He reopens the discussion of the two faculties by reasserting their likeness: fancy "is a younger sister of Imagination, without the other's weight of thought and feeling." Now, however, imagination is seen to be the primary Romantic creative force, and it is capable of finding a truth beyond the reach of man's purely analytical powers: "Imagination indeed, purely so called, is all feeling; the feeling of the subtlest and most affecting analogies; the perception of sympathies in the nature of things, or in their popular attributes."[30] By "feeling" Hunt means "intuition," as Thorpe reminds us.[31] Fancy, on the other hand, is only "a sporting with their resemblance, real or supposed, and with airy and fantastical creations."[32]

In Hunt's original definition, imagination is associated in his mind with the visual—"images of objects." By the time his definition is more fully developed, however, he qualifies that aspect by recognizing that fancy rarely has any "freedom from visibility." "The term Imagination is too confined" because it is generally seen as being "too material. It presents too invariably the idea of a solid body;—of 'images' in the sense of the plaster-cast cry about the streets."[33] This refinement indicates Hunt's strengthening of the power of imagination—the "analogical sympathy"[34]— at the expense of fancy, making his imagination less superficial in its similarity to Coleridge's shaping, or "modifying" faculty.

After a characteristic series of concrete illustrations, imagination emerges clearly as the force of "the more spiritual sympathies" and is seen as the property of the "serious muse," especially of tragedy; and fancy belongs chiefly to the comic.[35] Therefore, Hunt not surprisingly denies Pope any significant imaginative faculty but grants him fancy; on the other hand, Hunt applauds Coleridge's "exquisite" imagination and celebrates Shakespeare's balanced genius that "enjoyed the regard of both [imagination and fancy] in equal perfection."[36] In *Wit and Humour*, wit is defined by Hunt as "fancy in its most wilful, and strictly speaking, its least poetical state";[37] and he regards wit as an artificial combination of materials. Clearly Hunt shares what Myer Abrams calls Coleridge's "insistence on the distinction between the living imagination and the mechanical fancy,"[38] excluding as he does members of the "French school" from his anthology of "pure poetry."

Early in "What is poetry," Hunt sketches seven "different kinds and degrees of imagination," and these kinds range in a general way from manifestations of "everyday life" to more elevated and visionary forms.[39] By the time he is well into the essay, however, he admits that some new term is needed to replace "imagination"; for he apparently recognized the confusion resulting from the old and new associations clustered about the word. In *Biographia Literaria*, Coleridge had used the promising term "emplastic power" to explain his meaning of imagination, a term that unfortunately neither Hunt nor other contemporaries chose to adopt. Because of the immense significance of the imagination in relationship to Coleridge's esthetic theories, we may think it odd that there is no discussion of *Biographia Literaria* in Hunt's *Imagination and Fancy*, especially since, as Thorpe points out, Coleridge as poet is "the hero of the book—standing above Keats and Shelley, even above Spenser, as an exemplification of pure poetry."[40] Hunt's recognition of *Biographia Literaria* is limited to a short note at the end of his preface to acknowledge a coincidence between one page in Hunt's essay and Coleridge's study, a work to which he has just been reintroduced by a friend.

It is perhaps not so surprising, however, that Hunt makes no direct use of Coleridge's thesis. In his note, he warmly endorses the work; for he is as interested as usual in "extending the acquaintance of the public with a book containing masterly expositions of the art of poetry."[41] But Hunt, as he himself admits, is no scholar; his vague reference to Coleridge's work suggests a general rather than detailed familiarity. Furthermore, Coleridge's actual discussion of imagination and fancy is limited and fragmentary; his concluding paragraphs of chapter thirteen contain the chief passage treating the famous and puzzling distinction; but his promised major analysis never appeared. Clearly then, Hunt was not indebted to Coleridge for what had obviously become public property; and his ignorance of the book indicates the extent to which he had absorbed Romantic commonplaces.

Coleridge's distinction between what even as early as 1804 he called imagination's "modifying power" and fancy's "aggregating power"[42] is considerably more sophisticated than that proposed by Hunt, whose distinction was more in significance than in kind. Coleridge's fancy, "no other than a mode of memory emancipated from the order of time and space" and a part of the will, is contrasted, not simply with imagination, but with the "primary" as well as "secondary" imagination.[43]

But this more subtle and profound distinction is that of an esthetician, not of a teacher-critic. What is important for an appreciation of Hunt's work is the considerable area of agreement with his intellectual superior, albeit on the popular level. He recognized with Coleridge and other Romantic artists the supreme importance of imagination as man's primary creative power. In this realization, he falls somewhere between the extremes of Blake, who held the imagination to be the divine and only reality, and Byron, who acknowledged its power over him but seemed at times to fear it as a diseased faculty.

"Without imagination there is no true embodiment," Hunt asserts;[44] and he also reminds us by the way he ranks poets that he shares Coleridge's belief that imagination is essential for a good poem since fancy alone produces something less than "pure poetry." This belief explains Hunt's celebration of the Romantic achievement. Considering Coleridge as poet, George Watson points out that an often overlooked aspect of Coleridge's discussion of imagination and fancy is his conviction that "it is the decisive innovation of the Romantic poet to write imaginative poems rather than fanciful ones, just as it was the characteristic role of the Augustans to condemn themselves to a poetry 'addressed to the fancy or the intellect.' "[45] Certainly Hunt shared this view, both implicitly by awarding Coleridge, Keats, and Shelley three out of ten chapters in *Imagination and Fancy* and by placing them in the ranks of Spenser, Shakespeare, and Milton, and explicitly in his long war against Pope and the "French school." In *Imagination and Fancy*, this school is represented philosophically (and unfairly) by the earlier figure of Thomas Hobbes, who, like a child "educated on mechanical principle," could not understand how the imagination could produce an inner or imaginative reality.[46]

Hunt's ladder of seven kinds of imagination leads him eventually to a discussion of the "fabulous" and to a defense of fantasy. Consequently, the impression grows that for Hunt great poetry (i.e., the most imaginative) takes us away from reality and into a world of self-justifying art. However, as if having gone too far in the direction of some rootless world of imagination, Hunt pulls back to an imagination that works in the service of human truth. The poet "takes the world along with him" no matter how far beyond apparent reality he goes.[47] In heaven, it will be time enough for idealizing in a "superhuman mode"; now man should be "content with the loveliest capabilities of the earth." The healthy imagination of the Greeks allowed them to "imagine beyond imagination." Despite their myths, however, they returned the matter of poetry to the "only present final ground of sympathy—the human."[48]

Like Keats in his famous comparison of the imagination to "Adam's dream—he awoke and found it truth," Hunt argues the validity of this imaginative truth: "if it be asked, how we know perceptions like these to be true, the answer is, by the fact of their existence,—by the consent and delight of poetical readers."[49] Because of imagination, poetry is essentially "a passion for truth"—not only for the "subtle and analogical truths" but for "every kind" that belong to the poet by virtue of this faculty.[50] Hunt was convinced that much of the power of such writers as Chaucer and Homer resulted from their adherence to this "simplest truth." In describing their commitment, Hunt refers to their "passionate sincerity."[51] Like other contemporaries, Hunt is forced by the new attitudes toward creativity and art to use sincerity as a value judgment. In Hunt's shift from Wordsworth's use of the term to imply something like "artistic integrity" to the later Victorian use of the term to signify "emotional integrity," Hunt's usual application suggests more the Victorian than the Romantic position.[52]

But, while he believed in what Keats called "the holiness of the heart's affections and the truth of imagination,"[53] Hunt did not argue for the exclusiveness of such truth. The Romantic generation viewed science, that flower of seventeenth and eighteenth century rationalism, with mixed feelings; but its general position was not ultimately a hostile one. Science and art were felt by many to be "parallel and complementary ways of seeing," for each yielded its own kind of truth.[54] Analytical thinking was not, in itself, a bad thing; what was to be repudiated was the refusal to recognize other ways of knowing. Keats was a possible exception to this reconciliation. For, echoing an argument that he and Lamb had put forth at Benjamin Haydon's "immortal dinner" in December 1817, Keats in "Lamia" asks "Do not all charms fly / At the mere touch of cold philosophy?" For "philosophy will clip an Angel's wings" and, thanks to Newton, "unweave a rainbow."[55]

In Hunt's 1822 review of "Lamia," he rejects the fear that modern science has damaged poetry. In terms rather sharp considering his admiration and affection for Keats, Hunt rejects such an attitude toward science as "a condescension to a learned vulgarian"; and he curtly asserts that "a man who is no poet, may think that he is none, as soon as he finds out the physical cause of the rainbow; but he need not alarm himself:—he was none before." The "true poet" will ask "whether truths to the senses are after all to be taken as truths to the imagination," and he will recognize that the scientist's vision falls short of the artist's: "the essence of poetical enjoyment does not consist in belief, but in a voluntary power to imagine."[56] In *Imagination and Fancy* poetry is held to begin where science leaves off, and to "exhibit a further truth" because it taps the "world of emotion" and brings imagination to bear on the same material science employs. For the botanist to tell us that the lily is of the "Hexandria Monogynia" order is to tell us nothing. Spenser's " 'lady' of the garden" and Jonson's "the plant and flower of *light*" give us a "poetical sense of its fairness and grace" and show us "the beauty of the flower in all its mystery and splendour."[57]

Early in Hunt's career, he argued the superior didactic function of literature over history or biography in the "greatest part of what is called *the world*,"[58] and he might at any time in his career define the "moral" of a work. However, his faith in the didactic potential of art eventually assumed the Romantic rather than traditional form, whereas the reverse process was true for Wordsworth. Hunt, having come to share Keats' dread of poetry "that has a palpable design upon us," considered Wordsworth's "Peter Bell" to be "another didactic little horror . . . founded on the bewitching principles of fear, bigotry, and diseased impulse."[59] He was continuously concerned with the general intellectual and spiritual welfare of readers, but Hunt's was the Romantic faith in the moral imagination—the flowering of human sympathy—not in education by direct statement or by example.

One of the few extended quotations from another critic's theory found in *Imagination and Fancy* is borrowed by Hunt from Shelley's *Defense of Poetry*. "Poetry," quotes Hunt, "lifts the veil from the hidden beauty of the world, *and makes familiar objects be as if they were not familiar*": "the great secret of morals is love; or a going out of our own nature, and an identification of ourselves with the beautiful which exists in thought, action, or person, not our own. A man, to be greatly good, must imagine intensely and comprehensively; he must put himself in the place of another, and many others."[60] In short, he must develop the Romantic doctrine of empathy. In this development, Shelley writes and Hunt approvingly quotes that "the great instrument of moral good" is the "imagination; and poetry administers to the effect by acting upon the cause."[61]

The Romantic version of "instruction" Hunt happily calls "exhaltation," an appropriate term for the description of the truth of "spiritual sympathies."[62] Truth was posited by most Romantics, and particularly by Wordsworth and Coleridge, as the ultimate end of poetry. But "exhaltation" is the second of Hunt's "ends" of poetry; "pleasure" is the first. In this objective, Hunt is also in close agreement with Coleridge and Wordsworth; for, as Wordsworth asserted, "the poet writes under one restriction only, namely, the necessity of giving immediate pleasure to a human Being . . . ."[63] For Hunt, pleasure and truth are really one; however, it is "imaginative pleasure,"[64] despite his profound commitment to poetic truth, which chiefly concerns Hunt. Although he recognizes and always gives highest endorsement to the serious muse, we have seen in the last chapter that his anthologies and translations clearly illustrate his preoccupation with lighter, softer literature, especially the lyric and the sentimental narrative. His pleasure is often found in the richly if innocently sensuous; he is happiest in the world from which Keats struggled to escape, the realm of "Flora, and old Pan."

Hunt's lifetime addiction to books is repeatedly documented in his *Autobiography*. Especially after his two year prison term, his escape into the world of imaginative pleasure was frequent. Clearly, therapy was one of the principal uses to which he put literature, both as an artist and critic. At one extreme, this therapy could be found in serious or tragic poems through a sort of *felix culpa*. Following a quotation from *King Lear* that is rare in Hunt because of its painfulness—"Pray, do not mock me"—Hunt not only asserts that the elements of poetry make truth and beauty be seen as identical, but also that through their agency "pleasure, or at the very worst, a balm in our tears, is drawn out of pain."[65] This statement contains, of course, Hunt's version of tragic catharsis; but ordinarily he is more interested in pathos than in tragedy. The word "balm" points to the other extreme we have been discussing—that poetry, and literature more generally, to once again use Keats' expression, help to "sooth the cares" of men. If there is any pronounced weakness in Hunt as critic-teacher, it is in his assumption that this more superficial therapeutic value is what his readers need or want. It is the role of the teacher of literature to help his reader develop taste, and if poetry really does open human sympathies, as Hunt claimed, then a balanced taste in the teacher himself is necessary. Ultimately, Keats came to recognize (and to dramatize in his "Ode on Melancholy") the need to experience the coalescence of pain and pleasure; but Hunt refused to engage in the struggle that carried Keats to that point.

### III   *Romantic Theory: Unity, Metrics, Rhyme*

Just as Hunt generally reflects the Romantic doctrine of imagination and fancy, as well as the faith in the poetic truth that that doctrine was believed to produce, so *Imagination and Fancy* and other mature pronouncements declare his support or tacit acceptance (at some level of comprehension) of most other Romantic critical assumptions such as its views of unity. Although Romantic artists have often been accused of producing formless works, this charge frequently results from the critic's inability to recognize the nature of Romantic form, which in actual practice can be briefly described as non-Aristotelian, or organic. And, though there are well-known examples of Romantic fragments and works that lack either a traditional or a modern structural integrity, Romantic critical theory insists on the principle of unity. This insistence is especially true of Coleridge, who produced, under the influence of German philosophy, English Romanticism's most profound discussion of the theory of unity—Organicism.

As a critic, Hunt accepts the need for "oneness"; the idea is everywhere apparent in his work.[66] The power of poetry "modulates" and then "shapes this modulation into uniformity for its outline, and variety for its parts"; hence this "oneness" is "consistency, in the general impression, metrical and moral."[67] Hunt is close in this respect to Wordsworth's principle of "dissimiltude in simultude" that is stated in the preface to the *Lyrical Ballads*. Moreover, Hunt sometimes sounds almost as though he were aware of Coleridge's principle of the harmonious juxtaposition of opposites, of the synthesizing process that creative activity seems to involve, and perhaps even of Keats' sense of "making all disagreeables evaporate." For example, Hunt talks in the *New Monthly Magazine* (1825) about the "amalgamation of opposite feelings" and of the ability of "old poets" who, recognizing nature, are able to "reconcile" these opposites.[68] At times, Hunt even falls into the imagery of Organicism, such as when he argues that truth "can bud into any kind of beauty" through the creative power of imagination,[69] or when he states his theory that, following the passing of neo-Classical poetry ("like so many fantastic figures of snow"), spiritual growth began once more and "imagination breathes again in a more green and genial time."[70]

When Thorpe argues for the awareness in Hunt of the "elements of the Coleridgean concept" of Organicism, he admits, however, that Hunt never actually uses the term.[71] He points especially to the following statement in *Imagination and Fancy*: "Poetry, in its complete sympathy with beauty, must, of necessity, leave no sense of the beautiful, and no power over its forms, unmanifested; and verse flows as inevitably from this condition of its integrity, as other laws of proportion do from any other kind of embodiment of beauty (say that of the human figure), however free and various the movements may be that play within their limits."[72]

Yet, even on an unconscious level, Hunt is less aware of this principle of unity than might be apparent; for his "laws of proportion" probably reflect an earlier, more classical tradition since what he claims for art with "oneness" sounds something like the older demand for "decorum." His organizing principle is essentially static, and it appeals to an abstract, a priori notion of unity. The key to Coleridge's struggle to define Organicism lies in his awareness of the dynamic or emergent nature of form; it is the process of becoming. Although Hunt's inability to follow Coleridge does not invalidate his own apotheosis of the imagination, this incapability is a clear indication of the ad hoc nature of his critical precepts and of his intellectual limitations.

Hunt's "principle of Variety in Uniformity" or of "oneness of impression"[73] relates most closely to his insistence on the need for verse in poetry. To him, it is simply a "prosaical mistake" to argue that verse is not essential to genuine poetry as some have done; for "fitness and unfitness for song, or metrical excitement, just make all the difference between a poetical and prosaical subject."[74] The presence of verse provides evidence that the poet's "mastery over his art is complete," for verse illustrates his ability by "shutting up his powers in '*measureful* content'; the answer of form to his spirit." Although the verse form provides bounds for his creative freedom, it not only becomes no "clog," but is rather a positive help to the poet because it leads his creative energy into a "harmonious dance."[75] In this instance, we are reminded of Coleridge's "interpenetration of passion and of will, of spontaneous impulse and of voluntary purpose"[76]; and we recall his objection to Wordsworth's initial claim in the preface to *Lyrical Ballads* that "there neither is, nor can be, any *essential* difference between the language of prose and that of metrical composition."[77] Hunt shares Coleridge's conviction.

The importance of metrics to Hunt is made clear when we realize that the full title of his prefatory essay in *Imagination and Fancy* includes "Remarks on Versification" and that these remarks, though they involve a general discussion of poetry and much illustration, consume one-third of the space he allots himself for the education of his reader. Fine versification is seen to be the condition and requirement of fine poetry; and, to achieve fine versification, a poet must employ six qualities, each of which Hunt illustrates and discusses in some detail.

Of these six qualities that are essential to fine versification, "strength," which is neither "harshness," "heaviness" nor "weakness" ("want of accent and emphasis"), seems to suggest an essentially masculine quality: it "is the muscle of verse, and shows itself in the number and force of the marked syllables."[78] This quality is followed by "sweetness," a characteristic term of Hunt's that does not simply mean "smoothness," he at once assures us, since any hack can achieve that effect. Rather, "its main secrets are a smooth progression between variety and sameness, and a voluptuous sense of the continuous."[79] "Straightforwardness," a less purely connotative term, means essentially an adherence to natural word order; the opposite is not only the neo-Classical inversion but also "mere prose" itself.[80]

The quality "unsuperfluousness" is Hunt's cumbersome term for what he refers to as elsewhere as "economy," and only "pure barrenness" is more lamentable in a poet. Even true poets may be destroyed by "accumulation and ostentation"; anything unessential is "rubbish."[81] Hunt would surely have questioned Keats' famous advice to Shelley to "load every rift with ore"; and, in fact, he does criticize both Keats and Shelley for superfluousness.[82] "Variety," employed "for the prevention of monotony," makes use of "stops," "cadences," "emphasis," and "retardation and acceleration of time."[83] Hunt grumbles about "moderns" having lost the "more numerous versification of the ancients" and having therefore been forced into a limited choice between the regularity of the neo-Classical hexameter and the "one-syllabled notation of the church hymns."[84] In regard to this quality, Hunt takes the time to discuss with disfavor the "see-saw" of Pope and his fellow Augustans.

"Oneness," Hunt's final quality, firmly links metrics with the question of unity that we have discussed earlier; and to employ unity is, for Hunt, to ensure a "consistency, in the general impression, metrical and moral."[85] The unusually large proportion of space that Hunt devotes to versification in *Imagination and Fancy* corresponds to the position of importance it fills in his applied criticism; it is above all the texture of the poem that concerns him. He spends much less time disposing of the questions of poetic diction and rhyme. Pope, Thompson, and others are excluded from the anthology because of "that intentional, artificial imitation . . . which removes them at too great a distance from the highest sources

118

of inspiration";[86] this collection is, after all, to be a volume of "pure poetry." Hunt approves the use of rhyme, but he insists that it be natural and not simply employed for its own sake. It is, except in the drama and the epic, "one of the musical beauties of verse for all poetry" and Hunt never wearies of insisting that music is absolutely essential to poetry.[87]

## IV  Romanticism: Revolution, Nature, and Myth

Because revolution, nature, and myth connect Hunt with the uniqueness of the Romantic period, these three concerns deserve comment. The new men realized only vaguely their collective newness, for the word "Romantic" had none of the great if ambiguous significance it was later to acquire. Byron derogates the term, while others employ it very loosely (as does Hunt in his praise of the "essence of the romantic" in Keats) and imply no comprehensive identification. Contemporary labels like "Lakers," "Cockneys," and the "Satanic School" suggest a fragmentary view. Clearly, however, in the struggle against the eighteenth century and in the creative innovations produced by that struggle, there is a kind of self-identification. Central to this feeling was a strong realization that the political upheavals were not unrelated to the new poetry, at least to that of Wordsworth and the "Lakers." When Hazlitt brilliantly assessed his own period in *The Spirit of the Age* (1825), he found that "Wordsworth's genius is a pure emanation" of that spirit. His famous conclusion is that Wordsworth's muse is "a leveling one" and that "the political changes of the day were the model on which he formed and conducted his poetical experiments."[88]

Not only does Hunt recognize five of the six major poets of his age (overlooking Blake is understandable), but he also clearly perceives the revolutionary aspects of his period. In the preface to *Foliage* (1818), he traces the eclipse of the "French school" in part to "the political convulsions of the world, which shook up the minds of men, and rendered them too active and speculative to be satisfied with their commonplaces."[89] At least twice in 1821, we find Hunt speaking of "the great re-opening of the intellectual world by changes and revolutions":[90] "It remained for the French Revolution to plough up all our commonplaces at once; and the minds that sprang out of the freshened soil set about their tasks in a spirit not only of difference but of hostility [to eighteenth century esthetics]"[91] Prior to Hunt's crushing humiliation at the hands of

Byron in Italy, he prefaced his complimentary sketch of the famous
Byron and his work with a comment concerning the rarity of good
noblemen poets; most are ruined by the artificiality and ease of lives
filled with "readymade notions of superiority."[92] In short, for Hunt
too the muses are democratic. Hunt ranks with the most perceptive
critics of his age, not only in his rare ability to discern poetic
greatness but also in his sure sense of the uniqueness of the period.

Hazlitt and others recognized that not only social ferment but
new ways of seeing the natural world accounted for some of the
period's strangeness to traditional minds. "To the author of the
*Lyrical Ballads,*" for instance, "nature is a kind of home," Hazlitt
felt; and he even more brilliantly stated that Wordsworth "gathers
manna in the wilderness."[93] Hunt lacked his fellow essayist's
profound insight into what Wordsworth himself called the "active
universe," but he understood fully the period's general assumption
that the poetic sensibility either must make contact with the
physical world or must die like cut flowers in a glass of water, which
had been Pope's fate. In a nice paradox, Hunt declares that Pope
would have been a "better poet, had he had a stouter pair of
legs."[94] Love of nature and use of the imagination (always con-
nected in Hunt's mind), because they "are the two purifiers of our
sense," allow us to "hear all the affectionate voices of earth and
heaven."[95] Along with imagination and an acknowledgement of
emotion's role, "a sensitiveness to the beauty of the external world"
is one of the basic "properties of poetry."[96] In *Imagination and
Fancy* this sensitivity is seen as providing the necessary "conditional
truth to nature."[97]

As we have observed in Chapter 2, Hunt's own use of the natural
world, especially in his poetry, falls short of either the concrete
realization of a John Clare or the symbolic depth of a Wordsworth.
Depite Hunt's theoretical awareness, his is largely a "literary"
nature; he can never separate books from fields and groves; he
seems to regard literature as necessary to his appreciation of nature.
Moreover, his own evocations of nature often appear enameled, or
like scenes on Wedgewood plates. On the other hand, without
knowing Blake's "London" or Wordsworth's "parliament of
monsters," Hunt sensed that the cold separation of man from the
living world that was caused by urban life was a form of alienation
that weakened and that it reinforced other forms of alienation
against which modern man had to struggle if he were to survive.
Although Hunt was a city man who was most persuasive when

writing about the life of London, he was aware that urban life was organized artificially and that it lacked the organic integrity necessary to the spirit.

For Wordsworth, and to a lesser degree Coleridge, nature had an esthetic importance that had never before been recognized, for nature had become more than a primary source of subject matter or than something that had spiritual significance. In the general disorientation following the breakdown of the Enlightenment, nature provided Wordsworth with a symbolic orientation—psychic, social, cosmic—to give shape and significance to the poetic vision and to provide a necessary framework for larger poetic units. Indeed, the artist's struggle, even if a largely unconscious one, to provide a viable myth is perhaps the essence of Romanticism. Each of the major English poets sought his unique and only partially satisfactory metaphor to replace the dead one he had inherited. Although these metaphors provided at least a temporary equilibrium during which their greatest poetry was written, it is difficult to know how much of this central problem Hunt understood. Often his discussion of myth seems to ignore the larger unifying significance and to restrict itself to traditional conventions.

Whether or not Hunt recognized the attempts around him to construct new myths out of old ones, as in the case of Shelley and Keats, or new ones out of nonliterary materials, as in the case of Wordsworth, is not clear. Two facts, however, are clear: first, Hunt knew that a mythic dimension was necessary in art; for his discussion of this necessity is unsophisticated but unequivocal:[98] an esthetic structure depends in part on a symbolic frame of reference. To Hunt, we do not learn Greek legends as a "set of school-boy commonplaces," as a part of "mere scholarship," or as something that is simply decorative; instead, the Greek myth provides a kind of lens that enables us to penetrate the "essences" of nature.[99] In addition, Hunt recognizes that, on a lower level, myth may function as metaphor. In a statement similar to Wordsworth's note to the "Immortality Ode" (where he argues that he used the concept of preexistence "as a poet," not as a philosopher), Hunt defends Spenser's mythical landscape: "We must take his cosmography as we find it, and as he wants it; that is to say, *poetically*, and according to the feeling required by the matter in hand."[100]

Second, Hunt obviously recognized the mythological bankruptcy in that "very 'periwigpated' age in all that regarded poetry, from Waller down to the Doctor inclusive,"—a recognition shared by the young Wordsworth.[101] Correspondingly, Hunt continually celebrates the vitality of Renaissance myth, especially in the hands of Shakespeare and Spenser; and, among his contemporaries, he commends Keats for his use of mythic materials, perhaps since Keats' practice is similar to his own. He recommends his own poem "The Nymphs" as being "founded on that beautiful mythology, which is not one of the least merits of the new school to be restoring to its proper estimation" after the "frigid mistakes of the French school,"[102] whose use of myth was simply decorative and hence sterile. Romantic myth is indeed not one of the "least merits" of Hunt's contemporaries, but he here refers to a more literal renewal of interest in Classical myth. On this crucial issue, as on the question of nature, we must conclude that Hunt had come more than half way.

## V    *The Poet*

Hunt's view of the poet can be seen in his controlling definition of poetry as "the utterance of a passion for truth, beauty, and power, embodying and illustrating its conceptions by imagination and fancy, and modulating its language on the principle of variety in uniformity." The "means" of poetry is the whole universe; and the "ends" of poetry are "pleasure and exhaltation."[103] Although Hunt frequently shows a certain Romantic tendency to widen and soften the word "poetry" to include feelings that are never given artistic expression (and to use "poetic" to describe a variety of activities and sensibilities), in *Imagination and Fancy* he immediately distinguished poetry from the "poetic feeling which is more or less shared by all the world."[104] In this distinction he is similar to Wordsworth, who saw the poet as "a man speaking to men"; and this poet is distinguished from all men only by a heightened sensibility, not by a total difference in kind. This assumption underlies all of Hunt's criticism, theoretical and practical, since he has faith that the proper introduction to good poetry cannot fail to have its effect on the reader who is himself a kind of poet; indeed, the critic's obligation is to so stimulate the reader that his creative sympathies may be employed.

Hunt's definition of "the greatest poet" is that of the man richest in "thought, feeling, expression, imagination, action, character, and continuity";[105] and presumably every genuine poet possesses in some degree these qualities. Coleridge placed his emphasis on the poet as a synthesizing genius whose imagination was revealed in "the balance or reconciliation of opposite or discordant qualities. . . ."[106] Hunt recognizes this ordering power in the poet, but his emphasis is almost entirely upon the Expressive theory of poetry advanced by Romantic critics—upon the qualities of "utterance," "feeling," "expression." In such an adherence, he is perhaps closer to Wordsworth and his poetry of "spontaneous overflow of powerful feelings" than to Coleridge.

In *Imagination and Fancy*, Hunt repeatedly uses the word "passion" (which he glosses in a footnote as "*Passio*, suffering in a good sense,—ardent subjection of one's-self to emotion"[107]) to describe poetry's expressive nature and, as with his contemporaries, to illustrate the great shift in critical emphasis from the effects of a work on its reader to the creative act itself. This shift, as Abrams makes clear, introduces "a new orientation into the theory of art."[108] Hunt's poet, armed with and willing to rely upon his imaginative genius, is a culture hero whose spiritual and educational powers make him, in Shelley's famous words, one of "the unacknowledged legislators of the world." Hunt's ambition as a critic was to acknowledge that fact.

## VI  *Practicing Critic*

These and other loosely defined critical assumptions underlie Hunt's overwhelmingly numerous applied criticisms, reviews, prefaces, and introductions. But, if these ideas that Hunt helped popularize sound much "like a roll call of the chief Romantic critical ideas,"[109] as Thorpe, his kindest modern critic claims, they do not do so because they form a consistent, cohesive body of precepts. Although Hunt approached a work of art with certain working assumptions and expectations, they, whatever their nature, were modified by actual experience with works that affected him. He brought to each new work and to each new author the accumulated impact of what he had previously experienced; *Imagination and Fancy*, written late in his career, represents an empirically received set of assumptions. New works and new artists could produce in him the delight that springs from a high degree of receptivity, as well as from the kind of critical courage that allowed him to be at ease while taking a risk.

He knew that precept follows experience and that meeting an author on his own ground is the joy and the obligation of the practical critic. Hence, despite his occasional assertions of theory that culminate in *Imagination and Fancy*, Hunt's finest and most readily applied critical tool was close analysis; and he had mastered this approach early when he had begun to describe objectively the theater of his day, a task rarely attempted before him. His interest is always in the text: "I pretend to be no great scholar myself" he claims, "but what I do read, I read closely and with a due sense of what the poet demands."[110] Although he was speaking of his role as translator, this practice clearly applies to his critical technique. If we compare Hunt with many critics and reviewers of his day, such as Francis Jeffrey or William Gifford, we recognize at once his uniqueness in this respect. Sympathy with "what the poet demands" was a concept foreign to those critics who, possessing rigid critical principles, felt it was their duty to force the author to conform rather than for the critic to discover and encourage his uniqueness. With the partial exception of Hunt's firm esthetic and partly social doubts about the "French school," he is remarkably free of such bias. Nor is this freedom from prejudice only a matter of pure esthetics. The infamous critical attacks made on Keats and on Hunt himself as bad or as perverted authors were largely politically and socially motivated; for, in their critics' eyes, these members of the "Cockney school" with their liberal and democratic loyalties were automatically disqualified as artists.

To the extent, however, that Hunt shared (implicitly or explicitly) Romantic critical values, he was of necessity antiestablishment. This fact, coupled with his willingness to risk favorable opinion about authors as yet unsanctioned by the critical world, meant that his endorsement often illustrates not only his perspicacity but also his very real courage, especially in the early years of his defense and promotion of Shelley and Keats. If we argued, as some ungenerous scholars have, that Hunt's support brought these writers unnecessary abuse, we would have to recognize that he did not shrink from the vicious attacks made on himself as a result of his generous support. Since Hunt felt not only a teacher's responsibility to his readers but also a critic's responsibility to genius, his encouragement of emerging artists was at least as important to him as his encouragement of the new reading public.

When we consider the critical myopia of Hunt's great contemporaries, his ability to recognize and his willingness to acclaim the best poets of his era are utterly staggering. No major Romantic, not even Coleridge, can match his record; for, although his discovery of

Keats and Shelley remains a chief element in his literary fame, he also recognized and promoted the genius of Hazlitt and Lamb. Through a process of strenuous reevaluation, he finally recognized the unique superiority of Coleridge and, in a more qualified way, that of Wordsworth.[111] And the case of these two authors dispels the often repeated argument that Hunt instinctively sensed poetic merit.

Prior to being blinded to Byron's excellence by his shoddy treatment of Hunt and his family in Italy, Hunt was, with Shelley, one of the few writers of the day to grasp some of the immense value and significance of Byron's *Don Juan*. Although this record alone should be enough to secure our respect, we must not overlook the fact that Hunt was one of the very first to welcome and encourage not only Tennyson but also Browning when he was hardly an immediately popular figure. These major figures do not, however, exhaust the list; for Hunt was one of the first critics, for instance, to praise Coventry Patmore's early poems and one of the first Englishmen to perceive the genius of Stendhal.[112] The accuracy of these choices is the more remarkable if we remind ourselves how often the poets we now accept as major were ignored or condemned by the critics of their own time—and even by each other.

Hunt's surprising and often ignored record is further enhanced by the accuracy of his judgments concerning foreign and earlier English writers. Along with Lamb, Hazlitt, Coleridge, and others, Hunt played a significant role in the post-Enlightenment resurgence of Renaissance literature; nor was his taste restricted to the Shakespeare worship of his day, nor even to such luminaries as Marlowe and Spenser. Moreover, he served the cause of Chaucer and his age by never tiring of widening the modern reader's appreciation of the man who, for him, was the father of English literature. In addition to anthologizing and commenting on Chaucer, Hunt modernized sections of his work, as did several of his contemporaries. And if, as was the case with many prominent Romantics, Hunt was biased about Pope and his school, we can at least remind ourselves that such profound critics as T. S. Eliot were blind, in their revolt, about the real merits of their predecessors. Moreover, Hunt's genuine appreciation and understanding of Dryden's art partially compensates for his failure to recognize Pope's special genius.[113]

Nor was Hunt's taste in European literature less comprehensive.

It is often argued that his qualified enthusiasm for Dante is somehow a mark against his judgement. But even as a liberal Protestant and devotee of gentler literature, Hunt never failed to place Dante among the immortal artists of the Western world; in fact, he even declared in *Imagination and Fancy* the Italian's superiority to Hunt's beloved Spenser.[114] Beyond Dante, Hunt not only recognized the merits of a whole galaxy of continental authors but helped to support their English reputations. If Hunt's reading public was culturally insular, it was not because he did not try to encourage their cosmopolitanism. Indeed, we find in his frequent comparison and contrast of authors without regard to national origin the beginnings of what we now call "the study of comparative literature." He did not see, as many still apparently do, the need to isolate and compartmentalize the products of literary movements that clearly have international roots.

Hunt's good-natured receptivity to new artists and his catholicity of taste sometimes betrayed him into overenthusiasm for writers now forgotten or severely reduced in stature. As has been pointed out by unsympathetic critics, Hunt included John Hamilton Reynolds with Keats and Shelley in his famous "Young Poets" essay in the *Examiner;* and he found it hard to rate Charles Tennyson's poems lower than those of his brother Alfred in their joint volume. To some extent, this charge is just; but he soon began to recognize the huge difference in quality among the "young poets" and, dropping his support of Reynolds, he unflaggingly encouraged the other two. Moreover, a careful reading of Hunt's review of the Tennyson volume reveals that the critic gently but firmly singled out Alfred as the brother of greater promise.[115]

Hunt's policy was nearly always to be initially tolerant and hopeful, partly because he was a kind and genial man, and partly because he felt that the obligation of the critic (like the teacher) was to nurture whatever talent a writer possessed. But Hunt was not indiscriminate; for, as an example, Hunt in a review of the now forgotten James Bird's *The Emigrant's Tale* (1835), compliments Bird's carefulness of style and the "sunshine and warmth of a cheerful and benevolent heart," but he acknowledges that, despite these pleasant qualities, Bird's lack of "fancy and imagination" precludes his artistic greatness.[116] Appreciation of the best qualities in Bird, or in another weak poet like Thomas Wade,[117] in no way diminished Hunt's recognition and support of his great contemporaries.

In Hunt's anthology headnotes, reviews, and critical articles, he usually identifies the key to an artist's poetic character, to that which marks his peculiar quality. When Hunt is at his worst, his search produces such judgments as these about Shelley: the poet "is at once the most ethereal and most gorgeous"; "Nobody, throughout, has a style so Orphic and primaeval."[118] Hunt's problem is not only one of vague connotation but also one of sheer wrong-headedness that results from excessive love—one understandable but lamentable. This sort of description, starting with the Victorians, has always plagued Shelley; and Hunt significantly links his friend with the name Ariel. Hunt similarly describes Keats as one "born a poet," whose "thoughts were in a garden of enchantment, with nymphs, and fauns, and shapes of exalted humanity."[119]

Hunt's generalizations are usually much better than these examples suggest. For, responding to Keats' lines in "The Eve of St. Agnes" about Madeline "asleep in legends old," Hunt colorfully penetrates to what has been recently called "the metaphoric contract in poetry": Keats is "sucking the essence out of them [his poetic feelings] into analogous words, instead of beating about the bush for *thoughts*," which are not poetry.[120] Or, quoting again from Keats' "Eve of St. Agnes," Hunt argues that the lines show how "poetry, in its intense sympathy with creation, may be said to create anew, rendering its words almost as tangible as the object they speak of, and individually more lasting; the spiritual perpetuity putting them on a level (not to speak profanely) with the fugitive substance."[121] Both of these observations of Hunt's about the creative act are made for the benefit of "young students of poetry" as well as that of "young poets."

Typically, Hunt defines uniqueness through a considerable accumulation of concrete particularity, a practice we noted at the opening of this chapter. His emphasis is largely on style. Although he usually gives some attention to the artist's "thought," close attention to the work's texture really absorbs him; and Hunt usually demonstrates why he approves of a poem or a passage. For instance, when speaking of the modulation in a stanza of the *Faerie Queene*, Hunt quotes the stanza and divides it into its metrical pauses. Then he describes the quality of the pauses, accentuation, intonation of the vowels—all of which he sees as contributing to the success of the stanza.[122] In this discussion as elsewhere, Hunt's consideration of structure is noticeably absent; moreover, he provides almost no "reading" of the whole work. His search is for the author's essence, not for the work's thematic unity.

Because of the faddish, politically biased, and often introverted nature of much of the criticism written in Hunt's day, and despite his obvious deficiencies as both theorist and practitioner, Hunt makes refreshing reading. His significance for literary history lies in his usefulness as a popular index of the broad base of Romantic critical assumptions. His uniqueness and his more general value can be found in his enlightened critical motives — the desire to share pleasure and to promote the growth of taste—and in his methods, which, in the process of analysis and evaluation, place the work first.

CHAPTER 6

# Memorist and Autobiographer

IN 1850, with forty-nine years of vigorous, often stormy literary life behind him, Hunt released his *Autobiography*. This two volume life published by Smith and Elder had had, however, what amounted to its first edition in Hunt's ill-conceived and ill-fated *Lord Byron and Some of His Contemporaries*, published by Colburn in 1828. These two books utilize nearly the same materials, yet the *Autobiography* is the happiest and *Lord Byron* the most unfortunate of Hunt's longer works.

I   Lord Byron and Some of His Contemporaries:
*"Spleen and Indignation"*

As we are aware, after the short-lived *Liberal* folded and Byron at last sailed for Greece, the Hunts were left destitute in Italy, where they lingered precariously until rescued after Byron's death by the shrewd publisher Colburn. Returning to England in 1825, Hunt agreed to produce a major book for Colburn, who, having already published several volumes of Byroniana to meet a greedy market, persuaded Hunt to write yet another. When *Lord Byron and Some of His Contemporaries* was released in 1828, roughly the first third (and usually the only section read) actually dealt with Byron. The second third treated Shelley, Keats, and a number of lesser contempories; and the final third contained essentially what we now know as the *Autobiography*. Hunt's preface to the first edition of this book makes a queer, self-conscious defense of the work. After confessing that the book was originally intended to concern itself mainly with his own life and work, Hunt candidly admitted that his obligation to Colburn had induced him to add an account of Byron and other contemporaries. Arguing that his slowness in getting into print, despite the pressure to do so, proved his lack of desire to speak ill of the dead poet, he admitted that his "account is coloured,

128

though never with a shadow of untruth" by "spleen and indignation."[1] Moreover, he argues that he regrets the picture he has drawn of "the infirmities of Lord Byron, common or uncommon."[2] However, the second and cheaper edition that quickly followed in the same year included a more conventional, defensive comment about the Byron section. Since the book went unrevised into the second edition, it is difficult not to view as guilty protest and self-deceit Hunt's repeated use in the second preface of "sincere" or some synonym; the book had already outraged numerous readers; and immediately pirated editions in France and America had given Hunt even wider notoriety.

Hunt very briefly describes his English association with Byron and then moves to their Italian relationship. His intentions toward Byron are almost immediately obvious; for, by page thirty-four (of a 248 page sketch), Hunt is already implying that he had informed Byron himself of his opinions about him; hence, he is not going to say of the dead what he had been afraid to say to the living. By page forty, any equivocation is over; he begins a long series of accusations by frequently opening a paragraph with a damning generalization and following it with examples. Hunt's pent-up frustration, humiliation, and resentment appear in his views of Byron: he "had never known anything of love but the animal passion"; his books are "the best part of him"; he wrote *Don Juan* "under the influence of gin and water"; he "was so poor a logician, that he did not even provoke argument"; "he did not care for the truth." Byron "admired only the convenient and the ornamental"; he could not appreciate Spenser; he expected "money and fame" from the *Liberal;* his expedition to Greece was simply "in hope of another redemption of his honours"; he was "pleasantest when he had got wine in his head"; he "knew nothing of the Fine Arts, and did not affect to care for them"; his "love of notoriety was superior even to his love of money; which is giving the highest idea that can be entertained of it"; "his temper was not good"; "his superstition was remarkable"; "Lord Byron had no conversation, properly speaking"; "whether he was a man of courage" could be doubted; "Christian he certainly was not"; "the truth is, he did not know what he was; and this is the case with hundreds of people who wonder at him."[3]

We see in Hunt's evaluation of Byron's courage and conversational ability the extent to which his normal fairness and objectivity have been distorted by his reaction to Byron's injustice to him. Some years later, in reviewing a reprint of Boswell's *Journal of the Tour to the Hebrides*, Hunt confessed amusement (and implied amazement) at Boswell's candid report about his treatment by Johnson—his "lavish honesty" and his apparent lack of rancor in reporting his own humiliation.[4] Because Hunt's deeply wounded pride would not allow him to accept such an inferior position, he produced the most hostile book ever to be written by a close acquaintance of the famous poet. Although he could theoretically forgive Byron on the basis of his own belief in determinism and hence "the unhappy consequences of a parentage that ought never to have existed,"[5] Hunt could in practice forgive Byron nothing. Yes, Byron was "handsome," but "his countenance did not improve with age, and there were always some defects in it."[6] True, Lord Byron was an eminent man of letters, yet his "collection of books was poor, and consisted chiefly of new ones."[7] Something could be said of the beauty of his mistress La Guiccioli, but she in fact "was a kind of buxom parlour-boarder, compressing herself artifically into dignity and elegance, and fancying she walked, in the eyes of the whole world, a heroine by the side of a poet."[8] He cites Byron's quip to Hunt's eldest son Thornton that "he must take care how he got notions in his head about truth and sincerity, for they would hinder his getting on in the world,"[9] as a sign of an attempt at malign influence or at least sheer spleen; and he does not recognize in his rage that the clever boy was quite able to understand Byron's characteristic irony even if a prejudiced father would not. Hunt is even irritated by Byron's calling one of his servants "a sort of *Dolabella*" for his loyalty, "thus likening," Hunt sniffs, "a great simpleton of a footman to the follower of Antony!"[10] It was, of course, exactly the kind of observation that Hunt would himself make, always living as much in the literary as the real world.

Since the sketch produces the character analysis and the biographical tidbits that would fulfill the public's lust for details of the great exile's life, little attempt is made to analyze Byron's poetry. Hunt shrewdly recognizes *The Vision of Judgement* as "the best piece of satire Lord Byron ever put forth" and thinks it "the most masterly satire that has appeared since the time of Pope."[11] But Hunt evinces little enthusiasm for Byron's other work and much less for *Don Juan*. Juan "was a picture of the better part of his own nature," Hunt claims; and he then uses this comment as a springboard for another attack: "when the author speaks in his own person, he is endeavouring to bully himself into a satisfaction with the worse, and courting the eulogies of the 'knowing'."[12] In fact, Hunt here shows very little understanding of the complex nature of Byron's major work; and his earlier, less biased treatment of *Don Juan* had been both more perceptive and more enthusiastic.

Hunt never questions the rightness of his own conclusions. His one motive, he argues, despite the confession in his first preface, is to find and establish the truth of "Lord Byron's real history."[13] And, while he may, on occasion, lament "getting a little Gossiping," or feel forced to cry "O Truth! what scrapes of portraiture have you not got me into," he feels sure that "readers of good sense" will recognize his disclosures as "requisite to the truth of the picture."[14] In the first preface, Hunt claims two significant virtues: truthfulness and the lack of vindictiveness.[15] Lack of animosity is, of course, absurd; but there is a kind of validity in the first claim since Hunt really believes that all he writes is the truth—nor is his truth entirely a subjective distortion. Lady Blessington, herself a contributor to *Byroniana*, told Henry Crabb Robinson that "Leigh Hunt gave in the main a fair account of Lord Byron";[16] and, while some might question the word "fair," many modern critics would largely agree.

But, if the living bard had been widely denounced as revolutionary and immoral, the dead poet was rapidly becoming a national hero. Since he had died in a fight for freedom and since he was then Europe's most famous contemporary poet, much of the press once so hostile to Byron would now tolerate no attacks on his memory, especially those by his inferiors. Since Colburn, bent on profit from notoriety, released specimen pages in advance of publication and without Hunt's approval, Hunt had been soundly denounced by many influential reviewers by the time the popular edition reached the booksellers.

But, if Hunt failed in taste and judgment, and hence was unable to appreciate the paradoxical complexity of the man and his work, one strong claim may yet be made for his treatment of Byron. Both in his assessment and in his biographical account, Hunt *attempted* to set the record straight while Byron was still a part of living memory. Moreover, the final portion of his study is devoted to an interesting critique of other recent discussions of the poet. Although the effect of his work is often to debunk, the intention was to prevent additional growth of an absurd and distorted Byronic myth. That Hunt was not successful is only partly the fault of his approach, for the public sentiment was overwhelmingly against him.

At the end of the sketch, in a more charitable mood than that which often marks the body, Hunt makes this motive clear—not just for truth's sake but for Byron's: "Lord Byron has been too much admired by the public, because he was sulky and wilful, and reflected in his person their own love of dictation and excitement. They owe his memory a greater regard, and would do it much greater honour, if they admired him for telling them they were not so perfect a nation as they supposed themselves, and that they might take as well as give lessons of humanity, by a candid comparison of notes with civilization at large."[17]

In Hunt's first preface, he admits that Colburn's idea was to place the sketch of Byron first in the book, and that he had recognized such an organization to be a strategic error.[18] Indeed, with a different division and another title, Hunt might have escaped much of the acrimony he had to endure. For the tone of the work changes considerably when he leaves Byron and discusses Thomas Moore. Despite Moore's close alliance with Byron and his attacks on Hunt, his treatment of Moore is gentle in comparison to that of Byron. When, after his brief discussion of Moore, Hunt considers his beloved Shelley, the change in tone is still more striking. Byron had been celebrated by an international reading public; Shelley had been little read and greatly abused by the English. Hunt's essay on Shelley is much better, as Ian Jack reminds us, because his sympathy is with its subject; "Hunt was always at his best defending the under-dog."[19] In this section Hunt continues his lifelong battle for Shelley's recognition and appreciation; but he is sometimes capable of poor critical judgment. Shelley "was like a spirit that darted out of its orb, and found itself in another planet," Hunt tells us, thus exaggerating Shelley's otherworldliness into the classic Victorian misconception.[20] But in Hunt's struggle to achieve acceptance for the man as well as his poetry, he is usually correct and persuasive. He recognizes the chief aspect of Shelley's character to be what he calls "natural piety" and notes that, consequently, his behavior was marked by disinterestedness.[21] This selflessness, Hunt argues in a rare backward glance at Byron, contrasts with the great lord's desire to do "striking public things."[22] Despite the popular misconception, Shelley had "set his face, not against a mystery nor a self-evident proposition, but against whatever he conceived to be injurious to human good."[23]

Like Hunt's view of the man,[24] his response to Shelley's poetry is nearly always favorable; but Hunt, as we have already observed, considers the weakness in some of Shelley's poems to be "that they look rather [more] like the storehouses of imagery, than imagery put into action."[25] A poem Hunt especially enjoys, however, seems to him to be "sculptured and grinning, like the subject [Medusa]. The words are cut with a knife."[26] Hunt cites such anthology favorites as "Stanzas Written in Dejection Near Naples" as exemplifying two significant aspects of Shelley's poetic genius, "the descriptive and the pathetic"; but he admits that he should have liked to see such lyrics as this and "Love's Philosophy" an avocation only.[27] Shelley's real genius, he argues, was as a dramatist; he "ought to have written nothing but dramas, interspersed with such lyrics as these."[28] As proof of this assertion, he notes that Shelley's "completest production" was the *Cenci*.

Hunt's essay on Keats follows the pattern of the one about Shelley and shares the relaxed, gentle quality that characterizes most of the book after he had discussed Byron. We find, however, somewhat less warmth toward Keats and less than half the space devoted to him than was allotted Shelley. Despite Hunt's brevity, this sketch appears to have been the first published life of Keats. If Hunt's is less personal—Hunt and Keats had had an inevitable falling out before Keats had left England—his enthusiasm for Keats' poetry is apparent. In fact, a greater percentage of space than in the Byron and Shelley essays is devoted to discussion of Keats' poetry and with generally good results.

Hunt's critical method is again that of the "great introducer," a method we have seen him employ repeatedly in such works as *Imagination and Fancy*. Keats' "On First Looking into Chapman's Homer," which Hunt says "completely announced that new poet taking possession," is reprinted because the work is probably too little known and because Hunt can never resist spreading his board with such delights. He is at his critical best when he describes this poem as terminating "with so energetic a calmness," a phrase that surely captures the Keatsian essence.[29] Speaking of "The Eve of St. Agnes," which Hunt particularly admired, he "cannot resist repeating" two stanzas (twenty-four and twenty-five) "for the benefit of those who are not acquainted with" Keats' art since "the whole volume is worthy of this passage."[30]

We have confirmed the merit of these and nearly all other passages that Hunt reprints. When he generalizes, however, occasionally some of his old problems of taste emerge as, for instance, his failure to recognize a poetic vice partially learned from and partially shared with himself. Hunt describes certain critical problems in Keats' *Endymion:* "It was a wilderness of sweets, but it was truly a wilderness . . . of young, luxuriant, uncompromising poetry" that troubled those readers "accustomed to the lawns and trodden walks, in vogue for the last hundred years."[31] Such a wilderness troubled readers sympathetic to the new poetry too, including Keats himself. Hunt often shifts the blame from the esthetic failure of a contemporary poet to a general decline in taste that had been brought about by the eighteenth century.

We should remind ourselves that to support either Shelley or Keats in 1828, was not a common or popular activity. Hunt, however, has absolutely no doubt as to the immortality of these largely ignored or rejected poets. He will "venture to prophesy" the ultimate fame of Keats even more fervently than that of Shelley.[32] He supplies these details of Keats' life and art "which now look trivial, because his readers will not think so twenty years hence."[33] This prediction was a most accurate one; by 1848, when R. M. Milnes brought out his *Life, Letters and Literary Remains* of Keats, the poet had established himself as a major force in English poetry, and facts concerning his life were already in great demand.

The second volume of *Lord Byron and Some of his Contemporaries* opens with four brief chapters that discuss more than a dozen of his fellow writers. Of these writers only Lamb and Coleridge, both fellow Christ's Hospital graduates, have any major significance today. Not surprisingly, there is no mention of William Blake, but neither is there more than passing mention of Wordsworth. The discussion of Lamb, though very brief, is warm and anecdotal; it is obviously written with deep affection. Coleridge's treatment is more detached, but it firmly defends that great intellectual's abstract and introspective nature, and Hunt may have been responding to Byron's clever jibes in *Don Juan.* After Hunt's youthful attack on Coleridge and Wordsworth in *The Feast of the Poets*, his evaluation of their work fluctuated. Though on occasion he showed considerable admiration for Wordsworth, it was Coleridge who, in *Imagination and Fancy*, eventually was to epitomize for Hunt the genius of the new poetry.

Roughly, the final seven-eighths of the second volume is given over to "recollections of the author's life," a revision of which Hunt was to publish in 1850 as his *Autobiography*. As though Hunt were glad to have fulfilled the obligations incurred by his book's title and happy to be safely away from the center of controversy, the full measure of his grace returns. Nonetheless, this largest and most enjoyable section of the book ironically went almost unnoticed in the furor created by Hunt's attack on Byron. Although Morpurgo, in his introduction to the *Autobiography*, has described that work as being "in reality a magnificently arranged selection of journalistic writing,"[34] we remove the term "magnificently" in order to have a more accurate description of *Lord Byron and Some of his Contemporaries*. Indeed, very little unity, mechanical or organic, exists in this work. The opening section on Byron differs from the remaining two-thirds of the book in motive and tone; and the sketches that open the second volume have little connection with Byron, Shelley, and Keats. The concluding memoirs, despite their very real merit and biographical relationship to these three poets, actually function as anticlimactic and are seemingly unrelated material used to fill the volume. In short, this work is little more than a two volume miscellany of Huntian materials—another in his long series of anthologies—that indicates Hunt's dilemma: in a large work, his architectonic skill nearly always failed him.

Yet *Lord Byron and Some of his Contemporaries* has intrinsic value and deserves to be more widely read. First, the writing, when Hunt is not being petulant over Byron, is frequently up to his high standards. Second, Hunt's treatment of Byron, when viewed in light of our wider knowledge of the great poet, remains very useful in helping to evaluate his character and personality. Too many critics of Byron join Hunt's contemporary enemies in attacking Hunt's character rather than dealing with his observations on Byron which, though distorted, are valuable. Finally, the essays on Shelley and Keats, in addition to their historical significance, offer insights into their work by a critic who was not only one of the very first to recognize their worth but one who was also more often right than wrong in his literary judgments.

## II   *The* Autobiography: *Reluctant Chronicle*

The 1850 *Autobiography* actually follows something of Hunt's original plans for the 1828 edition. Before it became an assignment in Byron baiting, Hunt had hoped to publish a selection of his work prefaced by an account of his life. While the *Autobiography* is not an introduction to an anthology, Hunt indirectly incorporates many things that he had previously written; and he directly employs materials not only from the 1828 volume, but also from the *Ex-*

*aminer* and the *Liberal*.[35] Though Hunt was in 1850 a famous and respected man of letters, the first edition of his memoirs did not sell well. The second edition of 1860, however, revised and brought up to date by Hunt, and completed and published after his death by his son Thornton, went through a considerable number of printings in the next sixty years.[36]

The word "autobiography," rarely or perhaps never used in English before 1797, only gradually came into vogue in the early years of the nieteenth century. The form itself increased in popularity as the century wore on, and Hunt helped to accelerate public taste during the 1820s by republishing with Cowden Clarke good autobiographies from the past. Such a genre, in one form or another, was especially congenial to Romantic writers. It could take an exotic or highly abstract form, as in Thomas De Quincey's *Confessions of an English Opium Eater* or in Coleridge's *Biographia Literaria;* a poetic form as in the case of Wordsworth's *Prelude;* or a more conventional form in the hands of Hunt and others.[37] Leigh Hunt's talents seemed to lend themselves naturally to autobiography, because of his personal, colloquial style; his candid reference to himself in his essays; and his extensive involvement in the life of his period. Indeed, the vivacious, graceful, and nearly always interesting *Autobiography* is widely and justly considered the best of his book length works; but this book presents critical problems that include those dictated by the form itself and those chronic organizational problems found in all Hunt's longer works.

Problems inherent in the form Hunt recognized. Writing an autobiography, he confessed, "may not only be a very distressing but a very puzzling task, and throw the writer into such doubts as to what he should or should not say, as totally to confuse him."[38] Hunt chooses, as his book moves into his adult years, to focus on his literary life almost to the exclusion of his personal affairs; and, whenever possible, he turns to the discussion of other men. Thornton, in his introduction to the posthumous 1860 edition, saw this choice as a major feature of the book: "His Autobiography is characteristically pronounced in its silence. He has nowhere related the most obvious family incidents. The silence is broken almost in an inverse proportion to the intimacy of his relations."[39] Because "his whole existence and his habit of mind, were essentially literary," Thornton believed, the book was "less a relation of the events which happened to the writer, than their impressions on himself. . . ." "This characteristic of writing," Thornton added, "is in a great degree a characteristic of the man"; and the book may be actually more autobiographical, therefore, than it first appears.[40]

In Hazlitt's well-known portrait of Hunt in *Spirit of the Age*, he had described him as a writer who "runs on to the public as he does at his own fire-side, and talks about himself, forgetting that he is not always among friends."[41] Hunt himself admitted that he fell "more naturally into this kind of fire-side strain than most writers" because it had been his lifelong habit to assume an intimate, personal relationship with his readers, but he felt that perhaps this practice gave him a "greater excuse" to discuss himself than have most autobiographers.[42] Despite the general truth of these remarks, his approach to the *Autobiography*, if not its execution, was uneasy and self-conscious. Since he knew that the material would be associated with his unfortunate *Lord Byron* of twenty-two years earlier, he assures his readers that only the material from the previous book that "maturer judgement" had passed upon, was retained in the present volume.[43]

Obligations to Hunt's publisher, and perhaps the understandable temptation to "emphasize his desirability—and availability—as laureate," Fogle suggests,[44] drove him to produce the 1850 life. It was, in one sense, an easy book to write, since he had so much material ready at hand. Yet in the very first paragraph, he feels constrained to inform his readers that "a more involuntary production it would be difficult to conceive" and that its entertainment value depended on the kind of interest "which any true account of experiences in the life of a human being must of necessity contain": "I claim no importance for anything which I have done or undergone, but on grounds common to the interests of all, and to the willing sympathy of my brother-lovers of books."[45] Hunt is not simply being coy; for, as Blunden notes, had Hunt wished for publicity, he could have "surprised the public with the mere index of his literary, dramatic, musical, and political acquaintances" and, of course, enemies.[46]

When Hunt was contemplating an autobiography in Horsemonger Lane Gaol in 1813, he had assumed that just such a "mention of other names, better known, or worthier to be known" than his own would create the interest of such a volume.[47] He had also theorized that a private person's history "is of such a nature, that it might even be difficult to render it uninteresting."[48] Moreover, Hunt may have agreed with Coleridge who, defending "egotism" in modern poetry, argued that "the most interesting passages in all writings are those in which the author develops his own feelings."[49]

Yet Hunt is reluctant about speaking of events concerning himself and about implying any self-importance. Where, we wonder, is Hunt's side of the Skimpole story, his financial problems, his painful estrangement from Keats? At times, Hunt's withdrawal in a book in which he is supposed to be the chief subject is ludicrous; and we wince at such comments as "alas! wither am I going, thus talking about myself?"[50] Yet we recognize the sincerity of his reticence. Very near the conclusion of the 1860 edition, after citing a number of men that Hunt judges to be self-sacrificing and noble, he again returns to the theme of the first page:

Alas! how poor it seems, and how painfully against the grain it is, to resume talk about oneself after adverting to people like these. But my book must be finished; and of such talk must autobiographies be made. I assure the reader, that, apart from emotions forced upon me, and unless I am self-deluded indeed, I take no more interest in the subject of my own history, no, nor a twentieth part so much as I do in that of any other autobiography that comes before me. The present work originated in necessity, was commenced with unwillingness, has taken several years of illness and interruption to write, repeatedly moved me to ask the publisher to let me change it for another (which, out of what he was pleased to consider good for everybody, he would not allow), and I now send it a second time, and with additional matter, into the world, under the sure and certain conviction, that every autobiographer must of necessity be better known to his readers than to himself, let him have written as he may, and that that better knowledge is not likely to lead to his advantage.[51]

Keats had once claimed that he found a kind of smugness in Hunt,[52] and Hunt himself regrets "a certain tone of self-complacency" which may have marred the *Examiner*.[53] But the above passage illustrates Hunt's characteristic diffidence in the *Autobiography*; and even his rehearsal of what he calls the "cheerful ethics" of his *London Journal*[54] cannot remove his concern. Thornton attributed these doubts to an "ultra-conscientiousness" that caused Hunt to disclaim again and again any personal merit.[55]

As a result of Hunt's personal beliefs, the chief characteristic of the book is the modesty of its subject. He recognizes but does not emphasize either his role as a pioneer in modern dramatic criticism or the tremendous minority influence of the *Examiner*. Indeed, the discussion of his most famous periodical is slight, considering the significant role it played in both his and England's affairs. Nor does he overplay his role as political victim. Chapter XIV on "Imprisonment" would have been a perfect opportunity for sentimental melodrama or philosophic flight. However, the chapter opens with a fine sketch of Hunt's dour jailer Ives and maintains its charm throughout the description of his amazing domestication of his cell in Horsemonger Lane Prison. Hunt was, as Bernbaum aptly describes him, "a graceful martyr" to liberty and freedom of speech;[56] but, in recalling those events, he is just as graceful in avoiding a theatrical treatment of his martyrdom. He has no "quarrel, at this distance of time, with the Prince Regent," whose weaknesses he feels bound to pardon as he pardons his own faults.[57]

Having solved or ignored the difficulty of what to write about, Hunt was faced with his old problem of how to shape and to give unity to his materials. The play of Hunt's mind in the *Autobiography*, though not so very deep, is extremely wide in range; and it is this range of observation, not a detailed personal history, that Hunt wished to accomplish. Since Hunt had for several reasons less interest in the last twenty-five years of his life than in his earlier years, a chronological presentation would have been insufficient by itself to structure the *Autobiography*. As a result, Hunt's psychological rather than rhetorical logic is achieved by harnessing the associational process employed in his essays. In the chapter on "Playgoing and Volunteers" (VI), for instance, the section on actors and the stage is triggered very naturally by the presence of three actors in his regiment of St. James volunteers. But this device yields only page-by-page coherence. Properly subordinated, the method of narration creates mental verisimilitude; unchecked, it produces anarchy. Where the associational process fails, as it does occasionally in the book, the author's transitions become mechanical and abrupt.

More important than Hunt's use of the associational flow is his modification of time sequence with subject groupings. Like Wordsworth's *Prelude*, the *Autobiography* is organized on a topical as well as a chronological basis. In preparation for a discussion of his Italian experiences with Byron, Hunt includes a flashback chapter, a "Return to first Acquaintance with Lord Byron and Thomas Moore" (XVIII). Often the chapter headings clearly indicate this topical (but usually roughly chronological) organization: "Suffering and Reflection" (VIII), "Political Characters" (XI), "Keats, Lamb, and Coleridge" (XVI), "At Home in England" (XXIII), "Literary

Projects" (XXIV). Generally speaking, he is more chronologically
detailed and accurate in the chapters dealing with "Childhood"
(II), "School Days" (III, IV), "Youth" (V), and "Playgoing and
Volunteers" (VI). When he reaches maturity, the time sequence
assumes less and less importance as he moves, essaylike, through
broad areas that engage his mind and demand his observation. "By
thus arranging his materials by subject," as Law recognizes, "Hunt
succeeds in giving a particularly vivid and interesting impression of
his life" and that of the world in which he moved.[58] Hence, while
lacking great architectural strength, the book is much more effec-
tively ordered than most critics admit. Hunt's mind and temperament provide the natural unity; like the narrator of Byron's *Don
Juan*, Hunt himself gives the work its center.

Besides the additions and deletions of revision, Hunt added to the
first edition of 1850 only three new chapters to cover the interven-
ing twenty-two years since the publication of *Lord Byron*, and the
1860 edition contained only one more chapter—altogether perhaps
one hundred new pages. This slight treatment of his many mature
and prolific years indicates that, despite Hunt's usual commitment
to the future, his autobiographical interest lay in his early years.
There are probably two major reasons for such a slender increase.
First, since Hunt was one of those writers who, coming to public
attention early, never quite reached the mark that he or his readers
expected, the early years of his relative success preoccupy him. A second and perhaps more profound reason involves the immense
significance of Shelley to Hunt's life. From their meeting in 1816
until Shelley's death in 1822, the friendship was of paramount importance to Hunt; after Shelley's drowning, the memories of that
friendship remained sacred to Hunt for the rest of his life. The
effect of his greatest friendship on the *Autobiography* is well
described by Morpurgo. In revising the earlier memoirs,

Hunt made one vital change in emphasis. Whereas Byron is the central
diabolical personality of the earlier book, Shelley is the focus and the hero
of the *Autobiography*. Hunt's friendship with Shelley is both its climax and
its end. With Shelley drowned, the *Autobiography* is dead.[59]

Unquestionably, Hunt's account of the bleak years in Italy after
Shelley's death is flat when contrasted with his pride in the earlier
relationship and with his intense anticipation of the Italian venture.
Shelley's loss was a tragedy for Hunt in every sense; his best friend

was gone, his hopes for the *Liberal* were destroyed, and his energy was consumed. This second major crisis in his life was unlike the first one, his political imprisonment, for it left him far fewer reserves at its conclusion.

We also find a corresponding shift in Hunt's treatment of Byron. In his relationship with the famous poet, Hunt had made two public blunders. The first mistake had been in letting his excess gratitude allow him to dedicate *The Story of Rimini* to "My Dear Byron," thus opening himself to ridicule and abuse for suggesting an intimacy that did not exist. The second and more significant error was to allow his personal grievance to provoke him into a clearly biased attack on a famous and dead poet. In *Lord Byron*, Hunt had regretted the *Rimini* dedication;[60] but in the *Autobiography* he admits the error of his fruitless attack on Byron. He is sorry to have ever written "a syllable respecting Lord Byron which might have been spared."[61] Unlike the pretense of candor in the preface to the earlier work, he can be genuinely open: "I had prided myself—I should pride myself now if I had not been thus rebuked—on not being one of those who talk against others. I went counter to this feeling in a book; and to crown the absurdity of the contradiction, I was foolish enough to suppose that the very fact of my doing so would show that I had done it in no other instance!" "Such are the delusions," he adds, "of self-love."[62]

These statements are not simply a hypocritical preparation for another version of the original attack. He wishes his readers to be perfectly clear about his present assessment. "As I am now about to re-enter the history of my connections with Lord Byron," he tells us, "I will state in what spirit I mean to do it."[63] The treatment of Byron that follows remains critical, but the petty animosity and totally negative attitude are gone. This tolerance and this lack of rancour that (with the exception of his treatment of *Lord Byron*) are typical of the mature Hunt, everywhere mark the *Autobiography*. In the final chapter of the 1860 edition, Hunt refers to Charles Dickens as his "admirable friend,"[64] despite the pain Hunt had felt upon discovering himself cruelly and quite unjustly caricatured as "Skimpole" in *Bleak House*. He had considered and then rejected a plan to comment on this unfair portrait; but Dickens, while never openly confessing the satire, had shown every evidence of trying to make amends. Though in the 1850 edition Hunt had reprinted all of the famous *Examiner* article about the regent that had sent his brother and him to jail, in preparing the final edition he penciled it for omission; for his peace had been long since made with the royal family and with the government. Among all Hunt's old enemies, only the satirist William Gifford still provokes his unqualified contempt. Gifford is the sole man, he tells us, "I ever attacked, respecting whom I have felt no regret" since Gifford "had not a particle" of redeeming genius.[65] Hunt's concentration on the first half of his life and the gentleness with which he surveys the old battles produce what Jack calls the *Autobiography*'s "elegiac glow."[66] Dead are most of the numerous friends that had filled his earlier life, and the pleasant memory of deep affection softens and smooths the less happy relationships.

Much of the book is filled with portraits: Hunt's improvident though engaging father who preached perhaps too well; his mother, who "had no accomplishments but the two best of all, a love of nature and of books"[67] (a woman too shy to take guitar lessons from Benjamin Franklin); an eager Keats poised on the threshold of literary greatness; the beloved Shelley, whose lines in the *Revolt of Islam*, "I will be wise . . . and I was meek and bold," symbolize for Hunt the paradox of his character;[68] and numerous other people, some of whom now live only in Hunt's account.

And we have the emergence of Hunt himself—cheerful, optimistic, generous, impulsive, and fatally smitten with letters. As we review the details of his life we recall with him his early memories of a prison of the King's Bench and his parents' endless discussions of "politics and divinity." At school we find him refusing, like his friend Shelley, to be a fag; hoarding, savoring, and making presents of Cooke's British poets; worshipping Collins and Gray; reading and rereading Took's *Pantheon;* writing long and very bad imitations of Spenser, Pope, and Gray. At seventeen, through a subscription raised by his father, he publishes *Juvenilia*, his first book of poetry, which makes him a "kind of 'Young Roscius' in authorship."[69] We see him cutting his literary teeth on Voltaire, "the most formidable antagonist of absurdities which the world had seen";[70] we find him discovering the joy of playgoing and the burden of reviewing. His literary ambitions came early and were clearly marked: "my path was chosen before I knew them [influential friends]; my entire inclinations were in it; and I never in my life had any personal ambition whatsoever, but that of adding to the list of authors, and doing some good as a cosmopolite."[71]

So the portrait develops as Hunt, in Hazlitt's words, "runs on to the public." The picture gradually emerges of a man clearly from a lower intellectual and creative order than that of his great contemporaries, yet quite interesting despite his limitations. Hunt's mind, though of a very different quality from Byron's, plays associationally over human experience in a way reminiscent of *Don Juan*. As in his essays, Hunt has a habit of jumping from topic to topic but of making the shift seem natural and appropriate. In employing the word "delicious" to describe his friend Horace Smith, for instance, Hunt recalls Byron's objection to that use of the term. He then digresses for three-fourths of a page on the value of the word when applied to people—it is a tiny essay similar to his *Indicator* vein—before gracefully easing back to the subject of Horace Smith.[72]

Often the topic, Hunt discovers, stimulates an interesting observation. Discussing a period of illness when a friend, rather insensitively, took him to the laboratory of a surgeon to view his skeletons, Hunt contemplates the importance of these human remains on our consciousness. "The first sight revolts us simply because life dislikes death," Hunt says; then, in one of his modest flashes of insight, he adds that "the human being is jarred out of a sense of its integrity by these bits and scraps of the material portion of it."[73] On another occasion, discussing without anger the old charge against him of vulgar breeding, Hunt cleverly notes that in fact the "Cockney school of poetry is the most illustrious in England," for Chaucer, Spenser, Milton, Pope, and Gray were all city men like himself.[74]

But perhaps Hunt is most characteristic when he calls "friendship the most spiritual of affections,"[75] or when he repeatedly argues for a kind of *felix culpa* operative in the universe. Pain had taught him, he said, "that evil itself contained good"; moreover, a person may well "doubt whether any such thing as evil, considered in itself, existed."[76] He was ashamed of and hostile toward the concept of evil and the consequent threat of damnation in orthodox Christianity, and the *Autobiography* is infused with the liberal and Humanistic sentiments of his book of meditations, *Religion of the Heart: A Manual of Faith and Duty*, which he published in 1853. Hunt's innocent theories, marked chiefly by the importance of benevolence in man and God, contributed to conservative loathing of him as a free thinker. But, whatever the rejection of his less progressive contemporaries, these thoughts provided him with his life strategy: "the value of cheerful opinions is inestimable" since "they will retain a sort of heaven round a man, when everything else might fail him."[77]

Since optimism was central to Hunt's temperament, we find numerous indications that, after living well beyond his Romantic contemporaries, he eventually found much to his liking in the Victorian world. While he may lament some developments—for instance, the growth of prudery in language[78]—he is willing to join the swelling choir of praise for this "strong Saxon people, who have carried the world before them."[79] Admiring Italy as he does, he can yet be smug about the inferiority of that country where "the rarity of a gentlemanly look in the men is remarkable."[80]

The democratic friend of Shelley and former scourge of the Prince Regent (though never an antimonarchist), Hunt now backs the crown: "I prefer a republic under a limited monarch, to a republic without one. It seems to me to promise better for order and refinement, and for security, against reactions, of progression itself."[81] Unaffected by the darker side of Victorian consciousness, his faith in "progression" is touching. His optimism never wavered, despite many provocations; and, even as he felt personally hopeful, so he felt confident in England's ability to show the world the way: "All mankind must be fused together, before they know how to treat one another properly, and to agree upon final good. Prince Albert's project for next year [the famous Crystal Palace of the 1851 Great Exhibition] is a great lift in this direction."[82] He was confident that English culture and technology would succeed.

In other, associated ways, Hunt illustrates his transitional character. Nature in his hands is not yet "red in tooth and claw," but no longer is it the spiritually interfused "Active Universe" of Wordsworth and Coleridge. All that is left in the *Autobiography* of the Romantic's vigorous apprehension of the natural world is a kind of literary Pantheism, charming "Arcadian idealism" to delight the fancy and make Hunt unsure as to which is more pleasant, the real woods or their pastoral treatment by great poets.[83] For Hunt, no inevitable conflict exists between Prince Albert's Crystal Palace and the "Arcadian idealisms" stimulated by an older, preindustrial England. His optimism, not unlike that of many Victorians, is a curious blend of faith in technologial progress; in philosophical idealism; and, at least in Hunt's case, in a kindly, hopeful temperament. The final paragraph of the 1860 edition, while not representative of his literary talent, illustrates this quality. Addressing readers as friends, he hopes, in his habitual manner, that we may

all meet on some future day among the vortex of living multitudes, the souls of the dead, where "all tears shall be wiped off from all faces"; or, in another view of futurity, before that time arrives, may we all meet in one of Plato's vast cycles of re-existence, experiencing the sum-total of all that we have ever experienced and enjoyed before, only under those circumstances of amelioration in the amount which progressive man has been made to look for, and with no necessity for the qualification of *errors excepted*.[84]

We do not feel when we read this passage that we have been in the company of a great mind, but the reader has no doubt of Hunt's comfortable grace, sweet gentility, and cheerful good will. The *Autobiography* is, as Carlyle believed, an "altogether human" book—the engaging life of an engaging man.[85] It is, in fact, one of the very best autobiographies of nineteenth century England.

CHAPTER 7

# *Afterword*

L EIGH Hunt's chief qualities as a man and as a writer are foreign to our skeptical age, yet attractive for perhaps that very reason. The mainspring of his character was his faith in human nature and in the cosmos itself; as a result, his personality is marked by a tenacious optimism rarely found today. Because of the difficulties in the life he lived, this optimism was necessarily as much the result of a kind of spiritual self-discipline as of natural enthusiasm; in his discussions, the word "cheerfulness" assumes some of the philosophic force of Coleridge's "joy." His personality as well as his convictions allowed him, despite painful experiences, to fully enjoy life; his deep generosity moved him to share that enjoyment with others. Hunt possessed a kind of informed innocence, the result of temperament rather than ignorance; and it is difficult to resist using "kindly," "tolerant," and "wholesome" when describing him. He was, moreover, vivacious and usually interesting. His writings reflect all these personal qualities and, as Hazlitt recognized, "he improves upon acquaintance."[1]

Yet our appreciation of Hunt depends upon accepting him only for what he is and claims to be. Despite his splendid human qualities, Hunt did not possess a major talent. Though he wrote in every genre, he was most successful only in those now carrying the least weight—the familiar essay and the autobiography. His optimism kept him safely back from the abyss that opened under many another author's feet, and it precluded his presentation of any serious vision. The vivacity so attractive in his poetry and in his sprightly essays never yields to the deeper lyric mode of his more famous contemporaries. His value is like that of many fine teachers: more a matter of encouragement than accomplishment; more a question of sympathy than example. What we can savor in his work, especially in his essays, is his easy grace, his gift of observation, and his generous spirit. The vein he is capable of mining has valuable but limited ore; the reader who accepts that fact is amply rewarded. What emerges from his work is the sense of a total and engaging literary personality, a strong and attractive presence which, in both its artistic and biographical manifestations, claims our interest, sympathy, and respect.

Hunt's historical significance is clear. As a poet, he freed the English line from the shackles of neo-Classical restraint. He was a pioneering drama critic and a reforming journalist. As a literary critic, he deserves credit for discovering and fearlessly asserting the greatness of Keats and Shelley when to do so was considered not only absurd but also professionally dangerous. In addition, he not only links two generations of English Romantic writers but also continues beyond them. A reflector, if not an originator, of the Romantic point of view, he provides a common denominator of its experience and values. Finally, though much harder to estimate, considerable evidence points to Hunt's important role in enlarging and shaping the taste of nineteenth century English readers and even writers. Like Mathew Arnold after him, Hunt recognized the significance and the needs of the burgeoning middle class. Unlike Arnold, he did not hold himself aloof and scold from an Olympian distance; rather, he worked for the growth of that class from within its ranks. Hunt was essentially a teacher; his impact on the imaginative, intellectual, and moral well-being of the broad center of English life was incalculable. In the twentieth century, Virginia Woolf described Hunt as a "spiritual grandfather" more civilized than her own grandfather, for Hunt was one of those "free and vigorous spirits who advance the world" and seem like friends out of the past.[2]

# Notes and References

## Chapter One

1. Expensive reprints of some of Hunt's better known volumes now are becoming available.
2. Thomas Carlyle, *Selected Works, Reminiscences and Letters*, ed. Julian Symons (Cambridge, 1967), p. 764.
3. Charles Kent, ed., *Leigh Hunt as Poet and Essayist* (London, n.d.), p. xi.
4. Edmund Blunden, *Leigh Hunt, a Biography* (London, 1930).
5. J. E. Morpurgo, ed., *The Autobiography of Leigh Hunt* (London, 1949), p. 22; hereafter cited as *Autobiography*.
6. C. H. Herford, *The Age of Wordsworth* (London, 1924), p. 82.
7. *Autobiography*, pp. 248 - 49.
8. *Ibid.*, p. 250.
9. *Ibid.*

## Chapter Two

1. Walter Jackson Bate, *John Keats* (Cambridge, Mass., 1963), p. 165.
2. *Autobiography*, p. 420.
3. *The Poetical Works of Leigh Hunt*, ed. H.S. Milford (Oxford, 1923), p. xviii; hereafter cited as *Poetical Works*. All quotations from Hunt's poetry are from this edition.
4. *Ibid.*
5. There were no genuine collected editions of Hunt's poetry in his lifetime. Even the 1860 edition, example, which Hunt edited before his death in 1859, omits many individual poems, all of his dramas, his political satires, and the bulk of his 1818 volume, *Foliage*. The most nearly definitive edition is Milford's, cited above.
6. Quoted by Leon Edel, *Henry James, The Treacherous Years 1895 - 1901* (Philadelphia, 1969), p. 17.
7. *Autobiography*, p. 77.
8. *Leigh Hunt's Literary Criticism*, ed. Lawrence Huston Houtchens and Carolyn Washburn Houtchens (New York, 1956), p. 130; hereafter cited as *Literary Criticism*.
9. William Hazlitt, *The Spirit of the Age*, (London, 1954), p. 290.
10. "The Nile," *Poetical Works*, p. 248.

11. *Granger's Index to Poetry*, ed. W.F. Bernhardt and K.W. Sewny (Morningside Heights, 1967), lists eighteen of Hunt's poems or selections in anthologies published from July 1960 to December 1965. However, several of these are translations; typically we find only three or four. Granger's 1961 *Index* listed thirty-six poems or selections.

12. Significant exceptions are W. J. Bate and Amy Lowell.

13. Quoted by Hunt in *Lord Byron and Some of his Contemporaries*, (London, 1828), I, 273. Hereafter cited as *Lord Byron*.

14. *Ibid.*, p. 270.

15. *The Complete Works of William Hazlitt*, ed. P. P. Howe (London, 1931), IX, 244.

16. *Autobiography*, p. 258.

17. *Ibid.*, p. 257.

18. *Ibid.*, p. 258; for an interesting discussion of this subject, see Ian Jack, *Keats and the Mirror of Art* (Oxford, 1967), Ch. 1 *passim*.

19. *Poetical Works*, p. 12.

20. *Ibid.*, p. 13.

21. *Ibid.*, p. 2.

22. *Ibid.*, p. 10.

23. *Ibid.*, p. 5.

24. *Ibid.*, p. 3.

25. *The Letters of Thomas Moore*, ed. Wilfred S. Dowden (Oxford, 1964), I, 390.

26. *Poetical Works*, p. 12.

27. *Ibid.*, p. 15.

28. *Ibid.*, p. 9.

29. *Ibid.*, p. 19.

30. This scorn-provoking couplet was included in a group of lines Byron had marked "beautiful." See *Poetical Works*, p. 674 and pp. 668 - 78 *passim* for his other annotations.

31. According to Keats, Hunt complained that "the conversation [in *Endymion*] is unnatural and too high-flown for Brother and Sister." *The Letters of John Keats*, ed. M.B. Forman (London, 1952), p. 86. In his preface to *Rimini*, Hunt directly echoes Wordsworth's arguments.

32. *The Letters of Percy Bysshe Shelley*, ed. Frederick L. Jones (Oxford, 1964), II, 108. Shelley's endorsement of "the familiar language of men" for poetry is also firmly stated in his preface to *The Cenci*, a work dedicated to Hunt.

33. *Poetical Works*, p. 26.

34. *Ibid.*

35. *Ibid.*, p. xxiv.

36. *Ibid.*

37. *Ibid.*, p. 27.

38. *Autobiography*, p. 258.

39. *Ibid.*, p. 109.

40. *Poetical Works*, p. 145.

41. *The Feast of the Poets* (London, 1814), p. 28.

42. *Autobiography*, p. 258.

43. *Ibid.*

44. Bate, P. 81.

45. Keats, *Letters*, p. 129.

46. Bate, p. 78.

47. *Poetical Works*, p. 39.

48. *Ibid.*, p. 48.

49. *Ibid.*, p. 50.

50. *Ibid.*, p. 40.

51. *Ibid.*, p. 44.

52. Douglas Bush, *Mythology and the Romantic Tradition in English Poetry* (New York, 1963), p. 176.

53. *Poetical Works*, p. 327.

54. *Ibid.*, p. 320.

55. *Ibid.*

56. *Ibid.*, p. 325.

57. Bush, p. 178.

58. *Poetical Works*, p. 326.

59. *Ibid.*, p. 228

60. R. H. Horne, *A New Spirit of the Age* (London, 1844), p. 230. Horne's title refers of course to Hazlitt's 1825 *Spirit of the Age*. Only Wordsworth and Hunt are treated by both critics. For a typical example of Hunt's lush and voluptuous mythological nature, see *Rimini*, III, 382 - 485.

61. Bush, p. 177.

62. See for example his treatment of Chaucer's "Pardoner's Tale" in "Death and the Ruffians," *Poetical Works*, p. 112.

63. *Ibid.*, p. 55.

64. *Ibid.*, pp. 66, 68.

65. *Ibid.*, p. 72.

66. Gifford is judged to have supplied both of these motives; *Literary Examiner*, XXIV (December 13, 1823), 369.

67. *Autobiography*, p. 215.

68. *Poetical Works*, p. xxvii.

69. *Autobiography*, p. 215.

70. *Ibid.*, pp. 214 - 15.

71. *Ibid.*, pp. 223 - 24.

72. *Poetical Works*, p. 151; all quotations are from the *Reflector* version (1811).

73. *Ibid.*, p. 152.

74. *Ibid.*

75. *Ibid.*, p. 145.

76. *Ibid.*

77. See for instance the preface to *Foliage* in *Literary Criticism*, pp. 129 - 42 *passim*.

78. *Ibid.*, p. 181.

79. *Ibid.*, p. 190.

80. *Ibid.*, p. 191.

81. *Autobiography*, p. 435.

82. *Poetical Works*, pp. 194, 204.

83. *Ibid.*, p. 199.

84. *Ibid.*, pp. 217, 208.

85. *Ibid.*, p. 209.

86. *Ibid.*, p. 194.

87. *Ibid.*, p. 685.

88. Blunden, pp. 266 - 67.

89. *Poetical Works*, p. 80.

90. *Ibid.*, pp. 81, 82.

91. *Ibid.*, pp. 82, 83.

92. *Ibid.*, p. 82.

93. *Ibid.*, p. 84.

94. *Ibid.*, p. 86.

95. *Ibid.*, p. 85.

96. *Ibid.*, p. 88.

97. *Ibid.*, p. 90.

98. *Ibid.*, p. 92.

99. *Ibid.*, pp. 684, 699.

100. *Ibid.*, p. 687. The lines were originally in the first version of Wordsworth's Ode No. XLV in "Poems Dedicated to National Independence and Liberty"; however, he later softened the passage.

101. *Ibid.*, p. 688.

102. Neville Rogers, ed., *Percy Bysshe Shelley, Selected Poetry* (Boston, 1968), p. 440.

103. *Poetical Works*, pp. 339 - 40.

104. *Ibid.*, p. 340.

105. *Ibid.*

106. *Ibid.*, p. 257.

107. *Ibid.*, p. 269.

108. *Ibid.*, p. 257.

109. *Ibid.*, p. 276.

110. *Ibid.*, p. 240.

111. *Ibid.*, p. 248.

112. Blunden, p. 119.

113. *Poetical Works*, p. 248.

114. *Ibid.*

115. *Ibid.*, p. 368.

116. *Ibid.*, p. 250.

117. *Ibid.*

118. *Ibid.*, pp. 250 - 51.

119. *Ibid.*, p. 251.

120. *Ibid.*

121. *Ibid.*, p. 283.

122. *Ibid.*, p. 284.

123. *Ibid.*, p. 310.

124. Blunden, p. 84.

125. *Poetical Works*, p. 294.

126. *Ibid.*

127. *Ibid.*, p. 293.

128. *Autobiography*, p. 257.

129. *Leigh Hunt's Dramatic Criticism*, 1808 - 1831, ed. Lawrence Huston Houtchens and Carolyn Washburn Houtchens (New York, 1949), pp. 133, 132; hereafter cited as *Dramatic Criticism*.

130. Blunden, p. 83.

131. *Autobiography*, pp. 440, 442.

132. Arthur Symons, *The Romantic Movement in English Poetry* (London, 1909), pp. 223 - 24.

133. Allardyce Nicoll, *A History of English Drama 1660 - 1900* (Cambridge, 1960), IV, 180, 181.

134. *Ibid.*, p. 181.

135. Quoted by Hunt in *Lord Byron*, I, 400, 405.

136. *Literary Criticism*, p. 139.

137. *Poetical Works*, pp. 434 - 38; all Hunt's poetic translations can be found in this volume with the exception of Tasso's *Amyntas*, for which the editor had insufficient space.

138. Quoted by R. Brimley Johnson, *Leigh Hunt* (London, 1896), p. 9.

139. *Literary Criticism*, pp. 138 - 39.

140. *Iliad*, xviii, 232 - 46; *Poetical Works*, p. 385.

141. Clarence DeWitt Thorpe, "An Essay in Evaluation," in *Literary Criticism*, p. 29.

142. So Rossetti wrote in his copy of Hunt's *Foliage;* quoted by Thorpe, *Literary Criticism*, p. 19.

143. See W. P. Friederich, *Dante's Fame Abroad 1350 - 1850* (Chapel Hill, 1950); R. W. King, "Italian Influence on English Scholarship and Literature During the Romantic Revival," *Modern Language Review XX* (1925), 48 - 63; 295 - 304; XXI (1926), 24 - 33.

144. *Poetical Works*, pp. xx, xix.

145. *Ibid.*, p. xix.

146. *Ibid.*, p. xx.

*Chapter Three*

1. *Critical Essays on the Performers of the London Theatres* (London, 1807), p. 1. Actually published in 1808; hereafter cited as *Critical Essays*. Note the conservative critical terms used by Hunt, the young reviewer.

2. *Autobiography*, p. 155.

3. *Ibid.*

4. *Ibid.*

5. Jeffrey A. Fleece, "Leigh Hunt's Theatrical Criticism," Doctoral dissertation, University of Iowa, 1952, p. 42.

6. *Dramatic Criticism*, p. 164; for a detailed account of the English stage as Hunt found it see Nicoll, IV, 1 - 57.

7. *Critical Essays*, p. xii.

8. *Ibid.*, pp. 48 - 57.

9. *Dramatic Criticism*, p. 45.

10. *Ibid.*, pp. 45, 47, 48.

11. *Ibid.*, p. 50.

12. *Ibid.*, p. 258.

13. *Classic Tales* (London, 1806), I, 64 - 65.

14. *Ibid.*, p. 65.

15. *Ibid.*

16. *Literary Examiner* (London, 1823), pp. 257 - 58.

17. *Ibid.*

18. *Dramatic Criticism*, p. 40.

19. *Ibid.*, p. 282;

20. *The Tatler* (January 26, 1831), p. 494.

21. *Dramatic Criticism*, p. 164.

22. *Ibid.*, p. 10.

23. Appendix, *Critical Essays*, p. 55.

24. *Dramatic Criticism*, pp. 270 - 76, 32 - 34.

25. *Ibid.*, p. vii.

26. *Ibid.*, p. 38.

27. Louis Landré, "Leigh Hunt: His Contribution to English Romanticism," *Keats-Shelley Journal*, VIII (1959), 138.

28. *Classic Tales*, I, 65.

29. *Dramatic Criticism*, p. 207.

30. *Ibid.*, p. 173.

31. *Ibid.*, pp. 134 - 35.

32. *Ibid.*, p. 65.

33. *The Tatler* (March 21, 1831), p. 677.

34. *Dramatic Criticism*, p. 173.

35. *Edinburgh Review*, 28 (August 1817), 472.

36. *Dramatic Criticism*, p. 168.

37. *Ibid.*, pp. 317 - 18. See, for example, *The Examiner* (April 18, 1819; March 19, 1820) for favorable reviews of Hazlitt's *Lectures on the English Comic Poets* and *Lectures on the Age of Elizabeth.*

38. *Dramatic Criticism*, p. 291.

39. *Ibid.*, p. viii.

40. See R. W. Babcock, *The Genesis of Shakespeare Idolatry, 1766 - 1799* (Chapel Hill, 1931).

41. Jeffrey A. Fleece, "Leigh Hunt's Shakespearean Criticism," in *Essays in Honor of Walter Clyde Curry* (Nashville, 1954), pp. 181, 188 - 89.

42. *The Indicator,* 30 (May 3, 1820), 234 - 35.

43. *Dramatic Criticism,* p. 39.

44. George Dumas Stout, "Leigh Hunt's Shakespeare: A 'Romantic' Concept," in *Studies in Memory of Frank Martindale Webster* (St. Louis, 1951), p. 17.

45. Hunt, *A Jar of Honey From Mount Hybla* (London, 1870), p. 154. First published in 1848.

46. *Dramatic Criticism,* p. 66.

47. Stout, pp. 22, 26.

48. *Dramatic Criticism,* pp. 290, 291.

49. *Ibid.,* p. 15.

50. *Ibid.*

51. *Ibid.,* p. 227.

52. *The Examiner* (April 5, 1818), p. 219.

53. *Dramatic Criticism,* pp. 181, 182.

54. *Ibid.,* p. 15.

55. *The News* (October 27, 1805); see also *The Examiner* (February 14, 1808), p. 108.

56. *The Examiner* (May 3, 1818), p. 284. L. H. and C. W. Houtchens argue that Hunt's "extended attempt . . . to establish Marlow's Jew as within 'the pale of human nature' has no parallel in Lamb, Schlegel, Coleridge, or Hazlitt." *Dramatic Criticism,* p. 322.

57. *Ibid.,* p. 116.

58. *Ibid.,* p. 195.

59. *The Examiner* (February 21, 1808), p. 125.

60. Thomas Babington Macaulay, *Critical, Historical, and Miscellaneous Essays and Poems* (New York, n.d.), II, 503. First published in the *Edinburgh Review* (January 1841).

61. For Hunt on Sheridan, see *The Examiner* (July 14, 1816), pp. 433 - 36, and his edition of *The Dramatic Works of Richard Brinsley Sheridan* (London, 1840).

62. Appendix, *Critical Essays,* p. 54.

63. *Ibid.,* p. 53.

64. *Dramatic Criticism,* p. 35.

65. *Ibid.,* p. 36; cf. Hunt's preference for Steele over Addison expressed in his *Autobiography,* p. 38.

66. *Dramatic Criticism,* pp. 52, 59.

67. *Ibid.,* pp. 59, 53.

68. *Ibid.,* P. 59.

69. *Imagination and Fancy; or Selections From the English Poets* (London, 1845), pp. 295 - 96. First published in 1844; hereafter cited as *Imagination and Fancy.*

70. *Dramatic Criticism*, p. 4.

71. *Ibid.*, p. 220.

72. *Critical Essays*, p. vi.

73. *Ibid.*, p. viii.

74. *Dramatic Essays by Leigh Hunt*, ed. William Archer and Robert W. Lowe (London, 1894).

75. Both actors are quoted by Blunden, p. 43.

76. Quoted by Blunden, p. 44.

77. *Critical Essays*, p. 50.

78. *Ibid.*, p. 51.

79. *Ibid.*, p. 53.

80. *Ibid.*

81. *Ibid.*, pp. 51 - 52.

82. *Dramatic Criticism*, pp. 112, 113.

83. *Ibid.*, p. 113.

84. *Ibid.*, p. 219.

85. *Ibid.*, p. 220.

86. *Ibid.*, p. 180.

87. *Critical Essays*, p. 2.

88. *Ibid.*, p. 3.

89. *Ibid.*, p. 16.

90. *Dramatic Criticism*, p. 298.

91. *Ibid.*, p. 77.

92. *Ibid.*, pp. 188 - 89.

93. Blunden, p. 24.

94. *Dramatic Criticism*, pp. 146 - 52, 185.

95. *Ibid.*, p. 275.

96. *Ibid.*, p. 261.

97. *Ibid.*, p. 333.

98. Theodore Fenner's *Leigh Hunt and Opera Criticism* (Lawrence, 1972) appeared after this study was initially completed. His examination of Hunt's musical criticism should be an important contribution to Hunt scholarship. See also E.D. Mackerness, "Leigh Hunt's Musical Journalism," *Monthly Musical Record*, LXXXVI (November-December, 1956), 212 - 22.

99. *Autobiography*, p. 136.

## Chapter Four

1. Marie H. Law, *The English Familiar Essay in the Early Nineteenth Century* (1934; rpt. New York, 1965), p. 38.

2. *Prefaces by Leigh Hunt*, R. Brimley Johnson ed. (1927; rpt. Port Washington, 1967), pp. 49, 50; hereafter cited as *Prefaces*.

3. *Ibid.*, pp. 61, 63.

4. *The Companion*, I (January 9, 1828), 6.

5. *Prefaces*, pp. 72, 71.

6. *Autobiography*, p. 421.

7. George Saintsbury, in *The Cambridge History of English Literature*, ed. A. W. Ward and A. W. Waller (New York, 1916), XII, 245.

8. *Literary Criticism*, p. 381.

9. Reprinted in *Shelley - Leigh Hunt: How Friendship Made History*, ed. R. Brimley Johnson (London, 1928), pp. 218 - 23.

10. *Literary Criticism*, p. 83.

11. *Prefaces*, p. 7.

12. *Ibid.*, p. 28.

13. *Ibid.*, p. 32.

14. *Autobiography*, p. 204.

15. *Ibid.*, p. 175.

16. Quoted by H. C. Baker, *William Hazlitt* (Cambridge, 1962), p. 198.

17. *Ibid.*

18. Ian Jack, *English Literature 1815 - 1832* (Oxford, 1963), p. 320.

19. Quoted by Carl Woodring, Introduction, *Leigh Hunt's Political and Occcasional Essays*, ed. Lawrence Huston Houtchens and Carolyn Washburn Houtchens (New York, 1962), p. 20. Text hereafter cited as *Political Essays*.

20. Quoted in *Autobiography*, p. 231. Originally published in *The Examiner* (February 28, 1812).

21. Woodring, Introduction, *Political Essays*, p. 17.

22. Jack, *English Literature*, p. 320.

23. *Autobiography*, p. 174.

24. *Prefaces*, p. 34.

25. *Ibid.*, p. 29.

26. Crane Brinton, *The Political Ideas of the English Romantics* (Ann Arbor, 1966), p. 207.

27. Woodring, Introduction, *Political Essays*, p. 36. Comments on Hunt's political beliefs found in this discussion are strongly influenced by Woodring's excellent prefatory essay.

28. *Autobiography*, p. 175.

29. *Prefaces*, p. 59.

30. *Ibid.*, p. 35.

31. *Ibid.*

32. See Woodring, Introduction, *Political Essays*, pp. 1 - 6, for a good brief description of the English political situation when the *Examiner* was initiated.

33. *Ibid.*, p. 6.

34. *Autobiography*, pp. 177, 199, 212.

35. *The Examiner* (April 1, 1810).

36. Woodring, Introduction, *Political Essays*, p. 41.

37. *Ibid.*, p. 32.

38. *Prefaces*, p. 59.

39. *Ibid.*, pp. 60 - 61.

40. *Ibid.*, p. 61.

41. Essays of Leigh Hunt, ed. R. Brimley Johnson, (London, 1891), p. xxvii.

42. Walter Graham, *English Literary Periodicals* (New York, 1930), p. 312.

43. Baker, p. 229.

44. For a list of Lamb's best known works which first appeared under Hunt's editorship, see Graham, p. 142.

45. Law, p. 56.

46. Desmond King-Hele, *Shelley: The Man and the Poet* (New York, 1960), p. 75.

47. *The Literary Examiner* (August 9, 1823), p. 93.

48. *Prefaces*, p. 11.

49. Law, pp. 161 - 62.

50. Hazlitt, *Complete Works*, XVI, 219 - 20.

51. *Prefaces*, p. 16.

52. *Ibid.*, p. 92.

53. *Ibid.*

54. *Ibid.*, p. 93.

55. *Ibid.*

56. *Ibid.*

57. *London Journal*, XXII (August 27, 1834), 176.

58. *Literary Criticism*, p. 273.

59. *Prefaces*, p. 100.

60. *London Journal*, IV (April 23, 1834), 28.

61. *Prefaces*, p. 41.

62. *Ibid.*, p. 94.

63. Johnson, p. 85.

64. *Selected Essays*, ed. Joseph Priestly (London, 1929), p. viii.

65. *Autobiography*, p. xiv.

66. *Prefaces*, p. 25.

67. For example, the preface to the *Reflector*, in *Prefaces*, p. 40.

68. *Ibid.*, p. 33.

69. *Ibid.*, p. 36.

70. *Ibid.*,p. 29.

71. Ernest Bernbaum, *Guide Through the Romantic Movement* (New York, 1949), p. 269.

72. *Autobiography*, p. 78.

73. *Ibid.*, p. 38.

74. *Ibid.*, p. 139.

75. *Ibid.*

76. *Literary Criticism*, p. 79.

77. *Classic Tales*, I, 56.

78. George Saintsbury, *The History of English Prose Rhythm* (London, 1912), p. 363.

79. *The Indicator*, II (October 20, 1819), 9.

80. *Classic Tales*, I, 55.

81. Law, p. 40.

82. Quoted by Johnson, p. 140. *The Examiner*, (March 28, 1824).

83. *Literary Criticism*, pp. 208, 212.

84. Law, p. 136.

85. *Selected Essays*, pp. 213 - 14.

86. *Literary Criticism*, p. 208.

87. Of the *London Journal* essays, Launcelot Cross says: "Indeed since Montaigne, the father of us all, no essayist has been so truly personal as Hunt." *Characteristics of Leigh Hunt* (London, 1879), p. 35.

88. Jack, *English Literature*, p. 322.

89. *Classic Tales*, I, 72.

90. *The Indicator*, LXIV (December 27, 1820), 89.

91. Although he is speaking here specifically of the "Wishing-Cap" papers, the statement applies generally. Quoted by Johnson in *Essays*, p. xxv.

92. Quoted by Blunden, p. 141.

93. "To my Friend the Indicator," *The Works of Charles and Mary Lamb*, ed. E. V. Lucas (London, 1903), V, 83; quoted by Hunt in *The Indicator*, LI (September 27, 1820), 402.

94. *The Indicator*, XIV (January 12, 1820), 105.

95. *The Indicator*, XXXVIII (June 28, 1820), 302.

96. *Selected Essays*, p. viii.

97. Woodring, Introduction, *Political Essays*, p. 69.

98. *The Indicator*, II (October 20, 1819), 11.

99. Law, p. 96.

100. Ernest A. Baker, *The History of the English Novel* (London, 1936), VII, 243.

101. *The Indicator*, X (December 15, 1819), 73.

102. Johnson, p. 116.

103. *Prefaces*, p. 133.

104. *Imagination and Fancy*, pp. 135, 136.

105. *Book for a Corner* (London, 1849), II, 234.

106. *Prefaces*, p. 135.

107. Leigh Hunt, *One Hundred Romances of Real Life* (London, 1888), p. 6. First published in 1844.

108. M. H. Abrams, *The Mirror and the Lamp* (New York, 1958), p. 134.

### Chapter Five

1. Amy Lowell, *John Keats* (London, 1925), I, 136.

2. *Literary Criticism*, p. 284.

3. *Ibid.*, p. 282.

4. *London Journal*, XVIII (July 30, 1834), 142.

5. *Literary Criticism*, p. 240.

6. *Dramatic Criticism, p. 168; Literary Criticism,* p. 240.

7. *Ibid.*

8. *Imagination and Fancy,* p. iv.

9. *Wit and Humour, Selected from the English Poets* (London, 1846), p. vii; hereafter cited as *Wit and Humour.* This justification was originally used in the preface to *Imagination and Fancy.*

10. Macaulay, II, 501.

11. George Saintsbury, *A History of English Criticism* (London, 1949), p. 356.

12. *Literary Criticism,* p. 139.

13. *London Journal,* XVIII (July 30, 1834), 142.

14. *Literary Criticism,* pp. 387 - 88.

15. *Ibid.,* p. 388.

16. *Ibid.*

17. On Hunt's hope for a liberal fruition of society, see "On Extending to the Poor Part of their Countrymen the Blessings of Education," *The Examiner* (March 27, 1814); reprinted in *Shelley - Leigh Hunt,* pp. 224 - 28 See also his review of "a new book worth knowing," *Necessity of Popular Education as a National Object,* in *London Journal,* XXXIII (November 12, 1834), 257 - 58.

18. *The Indicator,* XXIV, (March 22, 1820), 186.

19. Three other volumes were planned: "Poetry of Action and Passion," "Poetry of Contemplation," and "Poetry of Song, or Lyric Poetry."

20. Samuel Taylor Coleridge, *Biographia Literaria* (London, 1965), p. 51.

21. Stephen F. Fogle, "Leigh Hunt and the End of Romantic Criticism," in *Some British Romantics,* ed. James V. Logan, et al. (Columbus, 1966), p. 119.

22. *Imagination and Fancy,* p. v.

23. *Ibid.,* p. iv.

24. *Ibid.,* p. 150.

25. Coleridge, *Biographia Literaria,* p. 50.

26. *Dramatic Criticism,* pp. 132 - 33.

27. *Ibid.,* p. 18.

28. *Ibid.,* p. 60.

29. *Imagination and Fancy,* p. 2.

30. *Ibid.,* pp. 29 - 30.

31. *Literary Criticism,* p. 53.

32. *Imagination and Fancy,* p. 53.

33. *Ibid.,* p. 31.

34. *Ibid.,* p. 30.

35. *Ibid.,* pp. 31, 32.

36. *Ibid.,* p. 33.

37. *Wit and Humour,* p. 9.

38. Abrams, p. 169.

39. *Imagination and Fancy*, pp. 7 - 10.

40. *Literary Criticism*, p. 61.

41. *Imagination and Fancy*, p. vii.

42. Samuel Taylor Coleridge, *Collected Letters*, ed. E. L. Griggs (Oxford, 1956), II, 1034.

43. Coleridge, *Biographia Literaria*, p. 167.

44. *Imagination and Fancy*, p. 27.

45. George Watson, *Coleridge the Poet* (London, 1966), p. 126. Wordsworth used both classifications in all editions starting in 1815.

46. *Imagination and Fancy*, p. 17.

47. *Ibid.*, p. 19.

48. *Ibid.*, p. 20.

49. *Ibid.*, p. 4.

50. *Ibid.*, pp. 2, 5.

51. *Ibid.*, p. 5.

52. See Patricia M. Ball, "Sincerity: The Rise and Fall of a Critical Term," *Modern Language Review*, LIX (1964), 1 - 11.

53. *The Letters of John Keats*, ed. Maurice Buxton Forman (London, 1960), p. 67.

54. Abrams, pp. 308 - 09; Chapter 11 (pp. 303 - 12) contains a useful discussion of the Romantic attitude toward science.

55. *The Poetical Works of John Keats*, ed. H. W. Garrod (London, 1956), pp. 176-77.

56. *The Indicator*, LXIII (August 2, 1820), 341.

57. *Imagination and Fancy*, p. 4.

58. *Classic Tales*, I, 1.

59. *Literary Criticism*, p. 143.

60. *Imagination and Fancy*, p. 68.

61. *Ibid.*

62. *Ibid.*, pp. 1, 32.

63. William Wordsworth, Preface to the *Lyrical Ballads, in Poetical Works of Wordsworth*, ed. Thomas Hutchinson (London, 1950), p. 737.

64. *Imagination and Fancy*, p. 4.

65. *Ibid.*, p. 7. Hunt often expressed faith in other temporal forms of the doctrine that good springs from evil, especially in his analysis of the evolution of society.

66. *Ibid.*, p. 38 and *passim*.

67. *Ibid.*, pp. 2 - 3, 38.

68. *Literary Criticism*, p. 216.

69. *Imagination and Fancy*, p. 5.

70. *Literary Criticism*, p. 129.

71. *Ibid.*, p. 51.

72. *Imagination and Fancy*, p. 37.

73. *Ibid.*, p. 35.

74. *Ibid.*

75. *Ibid.*, p. 36.

76. Coleridge, *Biographia Literaria*, p. 206.

77. Wordsworth, p. 736.

78. *Imagination and Fancy*, pp. 38, 39, 40.

79. *Ibid.*, p. 42.

80. *Ibid.*, p. 43.

81. *Ibid.*, pp. 48, 49.

82. See Thorpe's discussion in *Literary Criticism*, pp. 47 - 49.

83. *Imagination and Fancy*, p. 49.

84. *Ibid.*, p. 50.

85. *Ibid.*, 38.

86. *Ibid.*, p. vi.

87. *Ibid.*, pp. 58 - 59; in his *Stories in Verse* (London, 1855) Hunt found it important to reprint "A Study in Versification" from the preface to his 1832 collection of poetry.

88. Hazlitt, *Spirit of the Age*, p. 132. For an excellent short study of the relationship between Romanticism and contemporary political revolution, see Myer Abrams, "English Romanticism: The Spirit of the Age," in *Romanticism Reconsidered*, ed. Northrop Frye (New York, 1963), pp. 26 - 72.

89. *Literary Criticism*, p. 129.

90. *Ibid.*, p. 640; see also *The Indicator*, LXX (February 7, 1821), 137.

91. *Ibid.*, p. 150.

92. *Ibid.*, p. 153.

93. Hazlitt, *Spirit of the Age*, pp. 133, 135.

94. *Literary Criticism*, p. 130.

95. *The Indicator*, XXIV (March 22, 1820), 189.

96. *Literary Criticism*, p. 130.

97. *Imagination and Fancy*, p. 18.

98. *Literary Criticism*, pp. 134 - 36.

99. *Ibid.*, p. 135.

100. *Imagination and Fancy*, p. 86; italics mine.

101. *Literary Criticism*, p. 134.

102. *Ibid.*

103. *Imagination and Fancy*, p. 1.

104. *Ibid.*

105. *Ibid.*, p. 3.

106. Coleridge, *Biographia Literaria*, p. 174.

107. *Imagination and Fancy*, p. 2.

108. Abrams, *Mirror and the Lamp*, p. 21; see especially Chapter 1.

109. *Literary Criticism*, p. 57.

110. *Ibid.*, p. 139.

111. See *Literary Criticism*, pp. 673 - 75, for a good short history of Hunt's opinions of Wordsworth; for a more detailed examination see Louis

Landré, *Leigh Hunt (1784 - 1859): Contribution à l'histoire du Romantisme anglais* (Paris, 1935), II, 144 - 46, 148 - 52.

112. See J. Deschamps, "A propos d'un centenaire: Leigh Hunt et Stendhal," *Stendhal Club*, I (July 1959), 273 - 79.

113. If, indeed, it is a failure. Modern taste seems, on the whole, to support the more reasonable Romantic objections to much Augustan literature.

114. *Imagination and Fancy*, p. 74.

115. *Literary Criticism*, pp. 344 - 71.

116. *London Journal*, LXXVI (September 12, 1835), 311 - 12.

117. *Ibid.*, LXXV (September 5, 1835), 302 - 03.

118. *Imagination and Fancy*, pp. 296 - 97.

119. *Ibid.*, p. 312.

120. *Ibid.*, p. 334.

121. *London Journal*, XLIII (January 21, 1835), 19.

122. *Imagination and Fancy*, pp. 81 - 82.

### Chapter Six

1. *Lord Byron*, I, vii; the first preface is included in this edition, pp. iii - xii. Hereafter cited as *Lord Byron*.

2. *Ibid.*, p. ix.

3. *Ibid.*, pp. 40 - 220 *passim*.

4. *London Journal*, Monthly Supplement (June 30, 1835), p. 207.

5. *Lord Byron*, I, 149.

6. *Ibid.*, p. 150.

7. *Ibid.*, p. 76.

8. *Ibid.*, p. 68.

9. *Ibid.*, p. 48.

10. *Ibid.*, p. 119.

11. *Ibid.*, pp. 91, 216.

12. *Ibid.*, p. 129.

13. *Ibid.*, p. 242.

14. *Ibid.*, pp. 21, 139, 65.

15. *Ibid.*, p. vii.

16. Quoted by E. J. Lovell, Jr., ed., *His Very Self and Voice: Collected Conversations of Lord Byron* (New York, 1954), p. xxix.

17. *Lord Byron*, I, 248.

18. *Ibid.*, p. xi.

19. Jack, *English Literature*, p. 367.

20. *Lord Byron*, I, 300.

21. *Ibid.*, p. 296.

22. *Ibid.*, p. 328.

23. *Ibid.*, p. 345.

24. There is little need to wonder how Hunt would have treated Byron had he, rather than Shelley, been married to Harriet and been the unwill-

ing cause of her death. Hunt is totally sympathetic with Shelley in this matter. *Ibid.*, p. 315.

25. *Ibid.*, p. 359.

26. *Ibid.*, p. 357. Much of Hunt's material for this section on Shelley came from his then unpublished review of Shelley's *Posthumous Poems* (1824).

27. *Ibid.*, p. 363.

28. *Ibid.*, p. 366.

29. *Ibid.*, p. 410.

30. *Ibid.*, pp. 428, 429.

31. *Ibid.*, p. 416.

32. *Ibid.*, p. 442.

33. *Ibid.*, p. 413.

34. *Autobiography*, p. xiv. The Morpurgo edition cited here and used throughout this study is based on Thornton Hunt's 1860 edition.

35. Morpurgo provides a useful appendix to his edition in which he shows relationships between previously published material and the 1850 life; *Autobiography*, pp. 496 - 98.

36. Although dated 1860, the second edition actually came out in December 1859. Stephen F. Fogle reports "some ten printings by the original publisher" by 1906, and reminds us that three scholarly editions have appeared in our own century; *Leigh Hunt's Autobiography: The Earliest Sketches* (Gainsville, 1959), p. vi. Both the *Autobiography* and *Lord Byron* have recently had facsimile reprintings by AMS Press.

37. See Jack's discussion in *English Literature*, pp. 363 - 66.

38. *The Autobiography of Leigh Hunt* (London, 1850), I, viii - ix.

39. *The Autobiography of Leigh Hunt*, ed. Thornton Hunt (London, 1860), p. xii.

40. *Ibid.*, p. iv.

41. Hazlitt, *Spirit of the Age*, 289.

42. *Autobiography* (1850), I, vii, viii.

43. *Ibid.*, p. ix.

44. Fogle, *Sketches*, p. vii. With Wordsworth's death the position was open but went to Tennyson.

45. *Autobiography*, p. 1.

46. *The Autobiography of Leigh Hunt*, ed. Edmund Blunden, (Oxford, 1928), p. vi.

47. *The Correspondence of Leigh Hunt*, ed. Thornton Hunt (London, 1862), I, 75.

48. *Ibid.*

49. *The Poetical Works of S. T. Coleridge* (London, 1835), I, vi.

50. *Autobiography*, p. 429.

51. *Ibid.*, p. 448.

52. Sick and frustrated, Keats was unkind. He had been fairer and more apt when he referred to Hunt of "the social smile" in his "Great Spirits" sonnet.

22 Notes and References2 165

2 53. *Autobiography*, p. 275.
54. *Ibid.*, p. 428.
55. *Autobiography* (1860), p. xi.
56. Bernbaum, p. 267.
57. *Autobiography*, p. 230.
58. Law, p. 214.
59. *Autobiography*, p. xxiv.
60. *Lord Byron*, I, 54.
61. *Autobiography*, p. 320.
62. *Ibid.*, p. 321.
63. *Ibid.*, p. 318.
64. *Ibid.*, p. 443.
65. *Ibid.*, p. 217.
66. Jack, *English Literature*, p. 368.
67. *Autobiography*, p. 22.
68. *Ibid.*, p. 263.
69. *Ibid.*, p. 113.
70. *Ibid.*, p. 143.
71. *Ibid.*, pp. 148 - 49.
72. *Ibid.*, p. 189.
73. *Ibid.*, p. 166.
74. *Ibid.*, p. 415.
75. *Ibid.*, p. 83.
76. *Ibid.*, p. 164.
77. *Ibid.*, p. 165.
78. *Ibid.*, p. 422.
79. *Ibid.*, p. 440.
80. *Ibid.*, pp. 393 - 94.
81. *Ibid.*, p. 399.
82. *Ibid.*, p. 395.
83. *Ibid.*, pp. 414 - 15.
84. *Ibid.*, p. 463.
85. Carlyle, p. 764.

## Chapter Seven

1. Hazlitt, *The Spirit of the Age*, p. 288.
2. Virginia Woolf, *A Writer's Diary*, ed. Leonard Woolf (London, 1953), p. 35.

# Selected Bibliography

PRIMARY SOURCES

There has never been published, and probably never will be, a complete edition of Leigh Hunt's work; indeed, much of it does not deserve reprinting. During the second half of the nineteenth century and early twentieth, the several collections that were published, usually contained choice essays. In recent years some individual works, such as his *Autobiography* and *Lord Byron*, have begun to appear in expensive reprint form. A major deficiency will be corrected when Professor David R. Cheney publishes his edition of Hunt's letters, a great many of which do not appear in Thornton's 1862 collection.

I. Useful modern editions of Hunt's works:

1. Autobiography:
*Leigh Hunt's Autobiography: The Earliest Sketches.* Ed. Stephen F. Fogle. Gainsville: University of Florida Press, 1959.
*The Autobiography of Leigh Hunt.* Ed. J. E. Morpurgo. London: Cresset Press, 1949.

2. Essays and Criticism:
*Imagination and Fancy; or Selections from the English Poets.* Ed. Edmund Gosse. London: Blackie and Son, 1907.
*Leigh Hunt's Dramatic Criticism, 1808 - 1831.* Ed. Lawrence Huston Houtchens and Carolyn Washburn Houtchens. New York: Columbia University Press, 1949.
*Leigh Hunt's Literary Criticism.* Ed. L. H. Houtchens and C. W. Houtchens. New York: Columbia University Press, 1956.
*Leigh Hunt's Political and Occasional Essays.* Ed. L. H. Houtchens and C. W. Houtchens. New York: Columbia University Press, 1962.
*Shelley - Leigh Hunt: How Friendship Made History.* Ed. R. Brimley Johnson. London: Ingpen and Grant, 1928.
*Prefaces by Leigh Hunt.* Ed. R. Brimley Johnson. 1927; rpt. Port Washington: Kennikat Press, 1967.
*Selected Essays.* Ed. Joseph Priestly. London: Everyman's Edition, 1929.

3. Poetry:
*The Poetical Works of Leigh Hunt.* Ed. H.S. Milford. Oxford: Oxford University Press, 1923.

II. Periodicals and first editions:

1. Periodicals edited and partially or entirely written by Hunt:

*The Examiner* (1808 - 1821)

*The Reflector* (1810 - 1812)

*The Indicator* (1819 - 1821)

*The Literary Examiner* (1823)

*The Liberal: Verse and Prose from the South* (1822 - 1823)

*The Companion* (1828)

*The Chat of the Week* (1830)

*The Tatler* (1830 - 1832)

*Leigh Hunt's London Journal* (1834 - 1835)

*The Monthly Repository* (1837 - 1838)

*Leigh Hunt's Journal* (1850 - 1851)


2. Chronological list of chief first editions of books written or edited by Hunt:

*Juvenilia; or, Collection of Poems, Written Between The Ages of Twelve and Sixteen.* London: J. Whitting, 1801.

*Classic Tales, Serious and Lively, With Critical Essays.* 5 vols. London: J. Hunt, 1806 - 1807.

*Critical Essays on the Performers of the London Theatres, Including General Observations on the Practice and Genius of the Stage.* London: J. Hunt, 1807 [1808].

*The Feast of the Poets, With Notes and Other Pieces in Verse.* London: J. Cawthorne, 1814.

*The Descent of Liberty, a Mask.* London: Gale, 1815.

*The Story of Rimini, a Poem.* London: J. Murray, 1816.

*Foliage; or Poems Original and Translated.* London: Ollier, 1818.

*Lord Byron and Some of His Contemporaries, with Recollections of the Author's Life and His Visit to Italy.* 2 vols. London: Colburn, 1828.

*Sir Ralph Esher; or, Adventures of a Gentleman of the Court of Charles II.* 3 vols. London: Colburn, 1832.

*The Poetical Works of Leigh Hunt.* London: Moxon, 1832.

*Captain Sword and Captain Pen; a Poem. With Some Remarks on War and Military Statesmen.* London: Knight, 1835.

*A Legend of Florence, a Play in Five Acts.* London: Moxon, 1840.

*The Palfrey; a Love Story of Old Times.* London: How and Parsons, 1842.

*One Hundred Romances of Real Life; Selected and Annotated by Leigh Hunt.* London: Whittaker, 1843.

*Imagination and Fancy; or Selections from the English Poets.* London: Smith, Elder, 1844.

*The Poetical Works of Leigh Hunt, Containing Many Pieces Now First Collected.* London: Moxon, 1844.

*Wit and Humour, Selected From the English Poets.* London: Smith, Elder, 1846.

*Stories From the Italian Poets, with Lives of the Writers.* 2 vols. London: Chapman and Hall, 1846.

*Men, Women, and Books; a Selection of Sketches, Essays, and Critical Memoirs, from His Uncollected Prose Writings.* London: Smith, Elder, 1847.

*A Jar of Honey from Mount Hybla.* London: Smith, Elder, 1848.

*The Town; its Memorable Characters and Events.* 2 vols. London: Smith, Elder, 1848.

*A Book for a Corner; or Selections in Prose from Authors the Best Suited to that Mode of Enjoyment; with Comments on each, and a General Introduction.* 2 vols. London: Chapman and Hall, 1849.

*Readings for Railways; or, Anecdotes and Other Short Stories.* London: Gilpin, 1849.

*The Autobiography of Leigh Hunt, with Reminiscences of Friends and Contemporaries.* 3 vols. London: Smith, Elder, 1850.

*The Old Court Suburb; or, Memorials of Kensington, Regal, Critical, and Anecdotal.* 2 vols. London: Hurst, 1855.

*The Poetical Works of Leigh Hunt.* Ed. Thornton Hunt. London: Routledge, 1860.

*The Autobiography of Leigh Hunt.* Ed. Thornton Hunt. London: Smith, Elder, 1860.

*The Correspondence of Leigh Hunt. Edited by His Eldest Son.* 2 vols. London: Smith, Elder, 1862.

SECONDARY SOURCES

1. Bibliographies:

COLLINS, R.L., et al., comps. *The New Cambridge Bibliography of English Literature.* Cambridge: Cambridge University Press, 1969. Vol. 3.

GREEN, DAVID BONNELL and EDWIN GRAVES WILSON, eds. *Keats, Shelley, Byron, Hunt, and their Circles.* Lincoln: University of Nebraska Press, 1964. This bibliography, including items from July 1, 1950, to June 30, 1962, should be supplemented by the annual *Keats-Shelley Journal* bibliography.

HANLIN, F.S., comp. "The Brewer - Leigh Hunt Collection at the State University of Iowa." *Keats-Shelley Journal* VIII, 2 (1959), 91 - 94.

HOUTCHENS, CAROLYN WASHBURN and LAWRENCE HUSTON HOUTCHENS, eds. *The English Romantic Poets and Essayists: A Review of Research and Criticism.* 1957; rev. ed. New York: MLA, 1966. Excellent assessment of Hunt studies as of 1966.

2. Biographies:

BLUNDEN, EDMUND. *Leigh Hunt: A Biography.* London: Cobden-Sanderson, 1930. Best general biographical study of Hunt.

JOHNSON, R. BRIMLEY. *Leigh Hunt.* London: Swan-Sonnenschein, 1896.

Useful for views on Hunt as journalist; but, like work of Monkhouse
(below), superseded by Blunden and Landré.

LANDRÉ, LOUIS. *Leigh Hunt (1784 - 1859): Contribution à l'histoire du
Romantisme anglais.* 2 vols. Paris: Societé d'édition, 1935. Detailed,
comprehensive, scholarly study of Hunt's life and work. Not
available in English.

MONKHOUSE, COSMO. *Life of Leigh Hunt.* London: Walter Scott, 1893.
Like Johnson's work (above), this life is based heavily on the
*Autobiography* and thus is of limited biographical value. Its Victorian
attitude, however, suggests the late century's view of Hunt.


3. Criticism:

BATE, WALTER JACKSON. *John Keats.* Cambridge, Mass.: Harvard University Press, 1963. Extremely just evaluation of Hunt's relationship with
Keats and his qualities as man, poet, and patron.

BERNBAUM, ERNEST. *Guide Through the Romantic Movement.* New York;
Ronald Press, 1949. Good, short general evaluation of Hunt.

BLUNDEN, EDMUND. *Leigh Hunt's "Examiner" Examined.* London: Harper,
1928. Useful for its discussion of the literary activities of Hunt's best-
known journal.

BUSH, DOUGLAS. *Mythology and the Romantic Tradition in English Poetry.*
1937; rpt. New York: Norton, 1963. Useful discussion of Hunt's role
in the revitalization of Classical myth.

FENNER, THEODORE. *Leigh Hunt and Opera Criticism: The Examiner Years,
1808 - 1821.* Lawrence: University of Kansas Press, 1972. Analysis of
a little-discussed side of Hunt's journalistic career.

FLEECE, JEFFREY A. "Leigh Hunt's Shakespearean Criticism." In *Essays in
Honor of Walter Clyde Curry,* pp. 181 - 95. Nashville: Vanderbilt
University Press, 1954. This and the following study by Fleece
provide a general view of Hunt as dramatic critic.

———. "Leigh Hunt's Theatrical Criticism." Doctoral dissertation, University of Iowa, 1952.

FOGLE, STEPHEN F. "Leigh Hunt and the End of Romantic Criticism."
*Some British Romantics.* Ed. James V. Logan, *et al.,* pp. 119 - 39.
Columbus: Ohio State University Press, 1966. Evaluates Hunt's role
as popularizer of Romantic critical concepts.

GRAHAM, WALTER. *English Literary Periodicals.* New York: T. Nelson,
1930. Discusses Hunt's impact on the growth and development of
literary magazines.

HAYDEN, JOHN O. *The Romantic Reviewers 1802 - 1824.* London:
Routledge, 1969. Discussion of Hunt as reviewer and an examination
of contemporary reviews of his writing.

HAZLITT, WILLIAM. *The Spirit of the Age.* London: Oxford University
Press, 1954. Short portrait by a brilliant contemporary.

HORNE, R. H. *A New Spirit of the Age.* London: Smith, Elder, 1844. Interesting view of Hunt from early Victorian perspective. Hunt and Wordsworth only two writers treated by both Hazlitt (above) and Horne.

JACK, IAN. *English Literature 1815 - 1832.* Oxford: Oxford University Press, 1963. Acute general study; includes incisive comments on various aspects of Hunt's literary activities.

LANDRÉ, LOUIS. "Leigh Hunt: His Contribution to English Romanticism." *Keats-Shelley Journal,* VIII (1959), 133 - 44. Brief and lucid overview. (Serious students of Hunt should see Volume 2 of Landré's study listed under biographies.)

LAW, MARIE H. *The English Familiar Essay in the Early Nineteenth Century.* 1934; rpt. New York: Russell and Russell, 1965. Includes a detailed discussion of Hunt's role in the development of the personal essay and an analysis of its Romantic character.

LOWELL, AMY. *John Keats.* 2 vols. Boston: Houghton Mifflin, 1925. Many useful passages concerning Hunt's influence on Keats and his literary quality generally.

MARSHALL, WILLIAM H. *Byron, Shelley, Hunt and the Liberal.* Philadelphia: University of Pennsylvania Press, 1960. Excellent analysis of the relationship between these writers and of the brilliant but short-lived journal they produced.

NICOLL, ALLARDYCE. *A History of Early Nineteenth Century Drama, 1800 - 1850.* 2nd. ed. 1955; rpt. as Volume IV of *A History of English Drama 1660 - 1900.* Cambridge: Cambridge University Press, 1960. Describes the condition and quality of the theater that Hunt reviewed; treats his own dramatic productions.

ROLLINS, H. E. *The Keats Circle: Letters and Papers and More Letters and Poems of the Keats Circle.* 2nd ed. 2 vols. Cambridge: Harvard University Press, 1965. Useful on Hunt's role as patron and his relationship with Keats and others.

STOUT, GEORGE DUMAS. "Leigh Hunt's Shakespeare: A 'Romantic' Concept." In *Studies in Memory of Frank Martindale Webster.* St. Louis: Washington University Press, 1951. Examines the Romantic assumptions of Hunt's Shakespearean criticism.

————. *The Political History of Leigh Hunt's Examiner.* St. Louis: Washington University Studies, 1949. Best account of Hunt's political writing in the *Examiner* and its results.

THORPE, CLARENCE DEWITT. "An Essay in Evaluation: Leigh Hunt as Man of Letters." In *Leigh Hunt's Literary Criticism,* pp. 3 - 73. Excellent if generous overall assessment focusing on Hunt as critic.

WARREN, A. H. *English Poetic Theory, 1825 - 1865.* Princeton: Princeton University Press, 1950. Ch. 6. Helpful in its examination of *Imagination and Fancy* and its place in contemporary poetic theory.

WOODRING, CARL R. "Leigh Hunt as Political Essayist." In *Leigh Hunt's Political and Occasional Essays*, pp. 3 - 71. The best short study of Hunt's political background, views, and writings.

# Index

The works of Hunt are listed under his name

173

**DATE DUE**

| | | | |
|---|---|---|---|
| | | | |
| | | | |
| | | | |
| | | | |
| | | | |
| | | | |
| | | | |
| | | | |
| | | | |
| | | | |
| | | | |
| | | | |
| | | | |
| | | | |
| | | | |
| | | | |
| | | | |

DEMCO 38-297